AT THE END
OF THE
WORLD

ALSO BY LAWRENCE MILLMAN

Our Like Will Not Be There Again

Hero Jesse

A Kayak Full of Ghosts

Last Places

The Wrong-Handed Man

Wolverine Creates the World

An Evening Among Headhunters

Lost in the Arctic

Northern Latitudes

Paris Was My Paramour

Fascinating Fungi of New England

Hiking to Siberia

I'll Dream You Alive

Giant Polypores & Stoned Reindeer

AT THE END
OF THE
WORLD

....

A TRUE STORY OF
MURDER IN THE ARCTIC

....

LAWRENCE
MILLMAN

THOMAS DUNNE BOOKS
St. Martin's Press
New York

THOMAS DUNNE BOOKS.
An imprint of St. Martin's Press.

AT THE END OF THE WORLD. Copyright © 2016 by Lawrence Millman.
All rights reserved. Printed in the United States of America. For information,
address St. Martin's Press, 175 Fifth Avenue, New York, N.Y. 10010.

www.thomasdunnebooks.com
www.stmartins.com

Designed by Kathryn Parise

The Library of Congress Cataloging-in-Publication Data is available upon request.

ISBN 978-1-250-11140-1 (hardcover)
ISBN 978-1-250-11141-8 (e-book)

Our books may be purchased in bulk for promotional, educational,
or business use. Please contact your local bookseller or the
Macmillan Corporate and Premium Sales Department at
1-800-221-7945, extension 5442, or by e-mail at
MacmillanSpecialMarkets@macmillan.com.

First Edition: January 2017

10 9 8 7 6 5 4 3 2 1

To the Memory of
Rachel Carson, Edward Abbey, John Muir,
Peter Freuchen, Barry Commoner, Elliott Merrick,
Frederica de Laguna, Ejnar Mikkelsen, Paul Shepard,
Bob Marshall, Wetalltuk, and Henry David Thoreau

Let your life be a counter-friction against the machine.

—Henry David Thoreau

If you don't live it, it won't come out of your horn.

—Charlie "Bird" Parker, Jr.

Look at me, for I am God.

—Peter Sala

AUTHOR'S NOTE

In this account of an obscure Arctic tragedy, I've used the Inuit spellings of names rather than the widely variable spellings that appeared in newspapers and Mountie Police reports at the time of the tragedy. For example, the Inuit never put a "u" after a "q," but some of the Mountie reports refer to Qarak as Quarak or even Quarack. I've also pluralized words the way the Inuit pluralize them, so one white person is a *qallunaak*, but several white people are *qallunaat*. Likewise, Inuk is the singular of Inuit, a fact that most writers don't seem to realize, because they constantly refer to a single Inuk as an Inuit. On the other hand, I've simply added an "s" to pluralize words commonly used in English, like *kamiks*. I've also added an "s" to pluralize the East Greenlandic monsters known as *qivitoqs* and *tupilaks* because those words have entered into English parlance, too.

AT THE END
OF THE
WORLD

A SORT OF INTRODUCTION

In my journeys North, I collect stories, and when I return home, I try to coax those stories onto paper. This coaxing may take a day, a week, or a month, but eventually the story agrees to be written down.

Not so a particular tragedy that occurred in a remote area of Canada's Hudson Bay in 1941: it was elusive, recalcitrant, and perhaps even hostile to my efforts to put it onto paper. I want to remain obscure, it seemed to be telling me.

Meanwhile, the present kept intruding on the past. "Hey," it would announce, "there's been another terrorist attack." Or it would say, "Isn't it time for another google or two?" It would follow me from place to place like a predator in pursuit of its prey. "Download me!" it would demand.

I was in a quandary. Not even my old pals Charles Darwin, John Muir, Aldo Leopold, and Henry David Thoreau, hard as they tried, could provide me with any help. Nor was the unsurpassing strangeness of the Hudson Bay tragedy itself capable of assisting me.

At last a so-called lightbulb went on in my head, and I realized I couldn't write about the past without also writing about the world immediately around me. In other words, the present. With this realization, I gave birth to the notes you're now holding in your hand. . . .

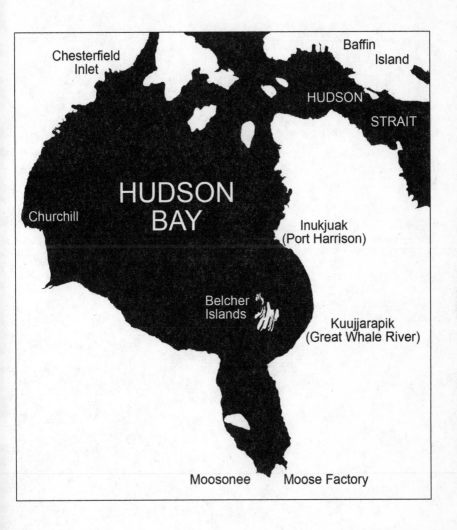

1

In 2001, I wanted to investigate the murderous aftermath of a meteor shower, so I flew from Boston to Montreal, then to Kuujuarapik in northern Quebec, and then to the Belcher Islands, a helter-skelter of fifteen hundred rocks in the turbulent waters of eastern Hudson Bay.

"I was afraid, I was so afraid," the old Inuit woman kept saying to me. Her hands were tightly clasped, and her eyes seemed to reach out and grab mine, as if she wanted me to see exactly what she had seen.

"You had to say, '*Ee, ee, the world is coming to an end*,' or they would kill you," another Inuit elder in the Belchers told me.

The world—in fact, more than one world—was indeed coming to an end.

2

From my notebook: I've pitched my tent at a place, Kingualuk, that consists of glacial rubble and till, boulders, and a sea of granitic pebbles. There's hardly a shred of pastoral softness here, only the earth's exposed bones.

And not just the earth's bones: the de-articulated bones of a Thule Period (AD 1100–1700) Inuk reside in a burial cairn on the hummock above my tent.

I once peered into a similar burial cairn in Hudson Strait and saw a wholly botanized skeleton, its every bone decorated with algae, lichen, and moss, whereupon I thought: *Green—what a splendid color to accompany one's journey to oblivion. . . .*

Near my tent, a seal skull and a walrus skull were resting so close together they seemed to be kissing. A reminder that all organisms both living or dead are connected.

Better a tattered notebook than a digital device for documenting this now rocky, now bone-ridden world. For a digital device would square and pixilate it, thus depriving it of its primordial delight.

I will nail my colors to the proverbial mast and say that I believe such devices are depriving us of far more than just primordial delights. . . .

We are a species that, in the words of poet Robinson Jeffers, likes to "break its legs / On its own cleverness," a fact that will occasionally oblige me to rant in these notes.

Example of a rant: Seated at a computer, you may think you're reflecting your own thoughts, but you're only reflecting your device's algorithms.

There were no algorithms at Kingualuk. Only the perpetual rhythms of the incoming and outgoing tides on rock.

A local Inuk named Simeonie told me this story: There was once a woman so ugly that no man would marry her. Rocks had no objection to her looks, so one of the rocks at Kingualuk took her for its wife, and they had a very happy life together.

I studied the rocks in the vicinity of my tent, but it was impossible for me to identify the wedded couple. Maybe all of them were wedded.

"Man is not above nature, but in nature," wrote nineteenth-century German biologist Ernest Haeckel.

Simeonie also told me about a mermaid with a typically Arctic morphology—part seal and part woman—who came ashore in the 1950s a mile or so from where I was camped. "I heard a visiting minister shot her," he said.

Another Inuk told me that it was a Hudson's Bay Company trader, not a visiting minister, who shot the mermaid.

Concerning the Hudson's Bay Company: it transformed the people of the Canadian North, formerly hunter-gatherers, into trappers, providing them with sugar, guns, ammunition, and the occasional mirror in return for furs.

"'Furs, furs, furs' is the white man's cry," wrote Arctic anthropologist Diamond Jenness in *People of the Twilight*.

Any reasonably intelligent mermaid who came ashore in the Belcher Islands during the winter of 1941 would have turned around and quickly swam back out to sea.

3

"Hudson Bay is a vast frozen sea that plunges like an icy wedge into the heart of North America," wrote Arctic historian Robert McGhee.

Lying in the southeastern part of Hudson Bay, the Belcher Islands were named after an eighteenth-century English sea captain who never set foot on them.

A series of pancakes, nibs, blunt teeth, and gable ends spread out over three thousand square miles, the islands may occupy a subarctic latitude (56° 20' N, 30° W), but their tundra habitat proclaims them resolutely Arctic.

The low-lying nature of the islands made early explorers and mariners give them a wide berth. Those few ships that didn't give them this sort of berth were invariably wrecked, like the *Kitty*, an English charter freighter that fetched up on the Precambrian rock outcroppings of the Belchers in 1859. . . .

. . . or the *Fort Churchill*, the main supply boat for the Hudson's Bay Company, which was wrecked off the islands' ubiquitous rocks in 1914.

Along with certain parts of New Guinea, Siberia, Antarctica, and the Amazon, the Belcher Islands were among the world's last remaining ends at the beginning of the twentieth century.

Question: Of what value is a map that doesn't have a blank spot on it?

In 1914, American filmmaker Robert Flaherty, then a mining prospector, asked a Canadian government official in Ottawa for permission to do some exploratory digging for iron ore in the Belchers. "There are no such islands," the official informed him.

The official may not have been altogether ignorant. After all, nonexistent islands are rather common in the North. Usually, they're large icebergs or mirages that occur when air layers of different densities sit on top of each other.

A year later, Flaherty found himself standing on the shore of Hudson Bay with an Inuk from Great Whale River (now Kuujjuarapik) named Nero. "Big land over there," Nero said, gesturing west in the direction of the Belchers.

Nero was not Nero's real name. Visiting *qallunaat* (white people, lit. "those who pamper their eyebrows") gave Inuit names that seemed to fit their personalities. Having learned to play the fiddle from a

Hudson's Bay Company trader named Harold Udgarten, the Inuk in question was named Nero.

Big land over there. These words gave the lie to the Canadian government official's earlier statement. So, too, did the words of an Inuk from Charlton Island named Wetalltuk, who told Flaherty: "I will draw you a map of those islands."

Wetalltuk had not been to the Belchers in twenty years, but his map of the islands is far more accurate than a map that Flaherty later drew to accompany an article he wrote for the *Geographical Review.*

So it was that Flaherty and his crew headed west from Great Whale River in a seventy-five foot topsail schooner called *Laddie.*

Just as the *Laddie* reached the Belchers, several kayaks came alongside it. Upon seeing the kayaks' eider duck skin–clad occupants, one of the crew, a man named Salty Bill, said to Flaherty: "Well, sir, some queer fish comes in with the tide."

Not surprisingly, the *Laddie*—like the *Fort Churchill* and the *Kitty*—smashed into the islands' rocks, and Flaherty and his crew were obliged to spend the winter of 1915–1916 in the Belchers. The *Laddie* itself provided him with most of his fuel.

Flaherty made two discoveries during his overwintering: that the islands' iron ore was of poor quality, and that the women were very compliant.

A local Inuk showed me an old telescope. "From my granddad's boat," he told me.

Apart from a flying visit by a Hudson's Bay Company employee named Thomas Weigand in the mid-nineteenth century, Flaherty was the first documented outsider to set foot in the Belchers. The main island is named after him.

Although I'm Gutenberg rather than Google, I recently googled "Flaherty Island," and one of my first hits was "Get Driving Directions to Flaherty Island."

Norwegian polar explorer Roald Amundsen called the Inuit "the happiest, healthiest, most honourable and most contented people" he'd ever met and said that he hoped "civilization may never find them."

Civilization did find the Belcher Inuit . . . and in a not necessarily pleasant way.

4

During his overwintering in the Belchers, Flaherty shot thirty thousand feet of film footage with a Bell & Howell hand-cranked motion picture camera, but he accidentally dropped a lit cigarette on the flammable nitrate-based film. The film ignited and was lost.

A few years later, Flaherty made the celebrated documentary *Nanook of the North* near the mainland village of Port Harrison. The film depicts a barely contacted group of Inuit very similar to the Belcher Inuit. Indeed, Flaherty's lost Belcher footage might be regarded as a tryout for *Nanook*.

The word Qiqiqtarmiut, as the Belcher Inuit call themselves, means "People of the Islands." A slight mispronunciation, and you'll get *qiqittaq*, which means "frozen feet" in Inuktitut, the polysynthetic Inuit language.

Nanook's real name was Allakarialluk. Flaherty didn't think cinema audiences would like such a hard-to-pronounce name, so he changed Allakarialluk's name to Nanook, which means "polar bear" in Inuktitut.

In the film, Nanook is a proverbial Noble Savage, a perpetually smiling primitive who knows nothing about white man's world, but in real life Allakarialluk was Port Harrison's postman, a man fully aware of that world.

Postman of the North is probably not a title that would have appealed to cinema audiences in either Flaherty's time or our own.

Nanook struggles to survive in a constantly harsh world, but Flaherty may have been more harsh to him than this world. In the journal he kept while making the film, Flaherty wrote: "Nanook's laziness reached a climax today. . . . Busted him, his pipe, and his tobacco in the snow."

So popular was *Nanook of the North* that its hero's likeness appeared on Eskimo Pie wrappers around the world all through the 1920s.

One of the film's most popular images shows Nanook listening to a record player with a mixture of bafflement and hilarity, as if he thought some sort of talking spirit inhabited this *qallunaat* box. A response many Inuit had when they first heard voices emerging from a record player.

Allakarialluk died shortly after the film was released. Flaherty announced that his hero had died of starvation, a condition much appreciated by the media.

In 2005, I visited Johnny Inukpuk, Allakarialluk's ninety-three-year-old cousin, who lived in the village of Inukjuak (formerly Port Harrison). During my visit, I mentioned that his cousin had starved to death. Johnny, who was flensing a seal at the time, nearly flensed himself.

"He died of tuberculosis," Johnny sputtered.

5

"To kill a culture," wrote Konrad Lorenz in *On Aggression*, "it is often sufficient to bring it into contact with another, particularly if the latter is higher or at least regarded . . . as higher."

Flaherty's visit meant contact with the outside world for the Belcher Inuit. A few of the islands' elders still describe events in the islands' history as being "before Mr. Flaherty" or "after Mr. Flaherty."

One consequence of first contact: popcorn. Flaherty introduced the local Inuit to it, "the most surprising thing by way of food they had ever seen," he wrote in his diary. At the time of my 2001 visit, they were still passionate about popcorn, which they called "gun food."

In the summer of 1919, the Royal Canadian Mounted Police made a visit, their first, to the Belcher Islands. The sergeant remarked of the Qiqiqtarmiut: "They are the most destitute people I have ever seen."

Possible translation of this statement: They were the most traditional people he had ever seen.

To these "destitute" people, everything had an *atiq* (soul). Birds, animals, plants, clouds, drift logs, rocks—all had souls. "In my grandfather's time, they even thought *anaq* (shit) had a soul," a local Inuk named Markassie told me.

A soul belonging to someone else—or something else—could enter a person and transform him or her, although that person would usually retain his human morphology. Thus your next-door neighbor could be a typical Inuk on the outside, but a bearded seal or an Arctic fox on the inside.

The notion that some sort of animal is hanging out inside you may seem primitive, but because it assumes you are just another organism, and that all organisms are related to each other, it's actually quite ecological.

"I believe in seals more than I believe in God," Markassie said.

Could what occurred during the winter of 1941 have made him somewhat suspicious of God?

6

By 2001, all 525 people in the Belchers were living in a village on Flaherty Island called Sanikiluaq, which was named after a local fast runner—a man who could outrun any animal he was hunting.

Immobility was, to Sanikiluaq, a terrible thing. He used to tell his children not to stand too long in one place, or something might come up from the ground and impale them.

Several of my informants were the grandchildren of Sanikiluaq, whom they affectionately called "Sani."

As I was writing up these notes, I googled "Sanikiluaq," and one of my first hits was "Cheap Flights from Sanikiluaq to Ho Chi Minh City."

Personal admission: Wherever I'm traveling, I refuse to carry a googling device with me. For I'd prefer to look at the world around me rather than stare at a screen.

At the time of my visit, there were some houses in Sanikiluaq that had televisions, but not indoor plumbing.

Flashback to Nain, Labrador, 1989: My Inuit guide exclaimed, "You're from Boston? *Ayee!! Cheers* is my favorite TV show." When I told him that I'd never watched *Cheers* or visited the *Cheers* bar, he gave me a look of complete bewilderment.

In the Belchers, even the old woman whom I said was so afraid owned a television, but mostly to inspire her grandchildren to visit her.

"When I was young, all we had was *unikkaaptuaq* [stories]," the old woman smiled. From this smile, I saw that a lifetime of chewing sealskins had worn down her teeth to a thin yellow ring resting against her gums.

Part of our survival as a species may have come from listening to stories, which entered our neural pathways and provided us with passed-on lore as well as passed-on entertainment . . . both un-interrupted by commercials.

Stories also gave us wisdom. In one Inuit tale, two men get into an argument over whether a seal pelt or a caribou pelt has more hairs, so they sit down and begin counting the hairs in their respective pelts, hour after hour, day after day. In the end, both men starve to death.

In 1828, Danish explorer Wilhelm August Graah read from a book of stories to a group of East Greenlanders, who bent down to listen to the book because, Graah wrote, "they thought that every word I read aloud to them . . . was communicated to me [from the book] in a whisper."

Just as plants, rocks, and animals had souls, they can talk, too. If you listen hard enough, you can hear them. Or so the Inuit used to think . . .

. . . just as they used to think that talking spirits inhabited record players.

I bent down to listen to the *Umbilicaria* lichens (otherwise known as tripe-de-roche or rock tripe) that decorated a boulder near my tent.

Was it my imagination or did I hear the lichens whisper, *Mercifully, there isn't any pollution in these parts?*

The more urbanized the place, the fewer the lichens. For they cannot tolerate the soluble particles from industrial pollution and automotive emissions that end up trapped in their thalli (vegetative tissue).

A few lichens seem to have triumphed over urban life. Recently, in Boston, I was studying a bright yellow *Candelaria* species on a tree when a little girl walked over and asked me what I was doing. Before I could tell her, her mother yanked her away, and then continued talking on her cell phone.

In 1941, there weren't any telephones in the Belchers, only a single highly erratic radio telegraph.

"Until ten years ago, I didn't own a telephone," a local Inuk named Taliriktuk told me, "so when I wanted to talk with someone, I would walk over to his house and talk with him."

Inuit names can be highly descriptive. For instance, Taliriktuk means "Strong Arm." The Qiqiqtarmiut called Robert Flaherty Soumik, which means "Tall, Left-Handed One."

My name was Allaut (pencil) because I was always writing in my notebook with a pencil.

A few years ago, I was sitting in a coffee shop in New York and writing in my notebook, and the man seated at the table next to me pierced the silence by barking into his cell phone, "So how'd the colonoscopy go?"

I asked the man not to talk so loudly. "My dad's hard of hearing, asshole," the barker said while gazing at his cell phone.

"The technology of human communication has advanced at blinding speed, but what people have to say to each other shows no comparable development," wrote Theodore Roszak in *The Cult of Information.*

"Just a guy staring at some weird yellow stuff on a tree," the woman with the young girl said to her cell phone.

7

From my notebook: An archetypal Hudson Bay gale, with the wind whistling at 50–60 mph. All planes are grounded. Likewise all birds . . . except a solitary raven performing playful maneuvers in the air above my tent.

Such windstorms, blowing west to east, can last for days, occasionally even weeks in Hudson Bay. "I am so used to the wind that when it stops, I fall over," a grinning Taliriktuk told me.

Once upon a time the Inuit believed that a strong wind was the voice of the weather spirit Sila telling them not to fear the natural world.

Message to Sila: Please get in touch with the twenty-first century's climate-controlled citizens and tell them not to fear the natural world.

Consider this paradox—the more climate-controlled the person, the more he or she complains about the weather.

In the words of a fellow Arctic aficionado, "If officials declare a state of emergency every time there's some snow, then the word emergency will lose all its pizzazz."

One evening I returned to my tent and found it blown almost flat against the ground, where it was vibrating like an accordion. A reminder that, in a place like the Belchers, Nature (permit me to capitalize it) invariably triumphs over human inventions.

A wolf spider (*Pardosa glacialis*) skittering around just outside my tent was quite pleased with the persistent winds. After all, those winds grounded flying insects and allowed it to suck out their delicious juices.

"Unto a life which I call natural I would gladly follow even a will-o'-the-wisp through bogs and sloughs unimaginable," wrote Henry David Thoreau in *Walden*.

Doubtless Thoreau would have followed that will-o'-the-wisp through winds unimaginable, too.

After I resurrected my tent, I did not re-inhabit it, but sat down outside and read Edward Abbey's *A Voice Crying in the Wilderness*, one of whose aphorisms I'll quote it here: "Belief in God? An afterlife? I believe in rock: this apodictic rock beneath my feet."

I was sitting on a similarly incontestable rock until a freezing rain began falling. It felt like a fistful of nettles on my exposed skin, so I retreated to my tent and listened to an obligato of the various elements playing on the tent's polypropylene.

One evening Markassie dropped by my tent and told me about an Inuk from the Belchers who'd lived his entire life in dwellings lit by seal-oil lamps. When he saw his first electric light at the Hudson's Bay Company post in Great Whale River in the 1950s, he cried, "Oh let it out, please let it out . . . poor light!"

During the long winter, light would have been such a precious commodity in the Belcher Islands that when a meteor shower flashed for an unusually long time across the night sky, it might have seemed like something other than a meteor shower to the Qiqiqtarmiut.

"Get ready for the future: / it is murder," sang Leonard Cohen.

8

The most dangerous book on earth," George Bernard Shaw called the Bible.

In the late nineteenth century, an English missionary, the Rev. E. J. Peck, translated the New Testament into Inuit syllabics in order to bring the Inuit, he declared, "the glad tidings of Jesus" and "give them a burning zeal for their salvation."

One of the Rev. Peck's Bibles somehow found its way to the Belcher Islands in the 1930s. The person who interpreted it to the other Qiqiqtarmiut was a man named Keytowieack. Over and over again, he emphasized the fact that Jesus was a very good person, and Satan was a very nasty one.

Keytowieack also quoted Matthew 24 from the Rev. Peck's Bible: "the stars will fall from the sky . . . and they [you] will see the Son of Man coming."

"I saw the pages of the Bible moving all by themselves, and then they stopped moving," the old woman told me. I asked her where they stopped. Perhaps the Book of Revelation? She looked thoughtful for a moment, then said, "I'm so old, I don't remember."

The Bible in question ended up being burned. For Jesus would provide each snowhouse with its own Bible when he arrived in the Belchers. Or so the Qiqiqtarmiut thought.

Nowadays, in Sanikiluaq, there isn't a resident clergyman. I asked the visiting clergyman about the events of 1941. "Past history," he said, then offered me a cup of tea.

Only elders were willing to talk to me, and then only certain elders. Others felt that what happened sixty years earlier made them seem embarrassingly primitive or, as one man told me, *isumairutivuq* [completely crazy].

"Those murders are like someone raping your daughter," a local Inuk told me. "You wouldn't go around talking about that rape, would you?"

The old woman asked me not to use her name if these notes were published. Markassie and Simeonie also told me not to use their actual names. But Taliriktut told me that he liked his name, and it didn't matter to him if I used it or not.

At present there's no actual mention of the tragic events of 1941 on the Belcher Islands website. All that website says is this: "RCMP [Royal Canadian Mounted Police] investigates incidents of violence."

"If you can't find it on the Internet, it's not worth knowing," an IT person recently told me.

The IT person in question was an inhabitant of Cyberia, one of the most highly populated realms on our planet. While Siberia possesses either endless taiga or endless tundra, Cyberia has no landscape, only endless screens.

Like Siberia, Cyberia has gulags, but the prisoners in those gulags can't hope for freedom because they don't realize they're in prison. . . .

Some of the activities commonly pursued in Cyberian gulags are cyberbullying, cybertheft, cybersquatting, cyberhacking, cyberstalking, cyberpiracy, cyberterrorism, downloading, and upgrading.

There is neither a past or a future in Cyberia, only the eternal present as purveyed by a screen.

Simeonie disagreed with the visiting clergyman. "Try to kill the past, and it will get stronger and more angry . . . like a polar bear you've shot and only wounded," he told me.

9

Once upon a time the Inuit believed that three sky-dwelling sisters made thunder, lightning, and rain. The thunder-maker was called Kadlu (Big Noise), the lightning-maker was called Kweetoo (She Who Strikes Fire), and the rain-maker was called Ignirtoq (She Who Pisses a Lot).

There was no sister who made meteor showers, but in an Inuit story collected by explorer Knud Rasmussen, a meteor shower descends from the sky and enters the vagina of a woman just as she was answering nature's call. At that exact moment, the woman became a powerful *angakok* (shaman).

During the winter of 1940–41, the hunting was very poor. There seemed to be no seals in the ocean and no freshwater seals in Kasagaluk Lake on Flaherty Island. No walrus or arctic hares, either.

Nor any caribou. They'd been gone since the 1880s, when a strange winter rain fell, then froze. The caribou could not scratch through the ice to reach the *Cladonia* lichens that were their winter food, and they starved.

"A girl in our camp had almost no food that winter, and she was nursing her baby," the old woman told me. "Her breast milk turned green, then dried up."

One night the sky above the Belchers was lit up by an especially long meteor shower, and the Qiqiqtarmiut took it as a sign. . . .

A twenty-seven-year-old man named Ouyerack regarded himself an *angakok*. He'd recently heard from Keytowieack about Jesus Christ, the white man's *angakok*, and he was envious of his, Jesus's, shamanic powers.

Like Jesus, Inuit *angakut* had the ability to raise the dead, but by Ouyerack's time, most of them seemed to have lost this ability. All the more reason to envy Jesus.

"Ouyerack was very short even for an Inuk," the old woman told me. She put her hand just below my shoulder to indicate that he was probably no more than five feet tall.

Shortly after the meteor shower trailed fire across the sky, Ouyerack shouted: "I am Jesus Christ! I am Jesus Christ!"

Ouyerack was not the first Inuk to identify himself as Jesus. In 1924, on Baffin Island, a man named Neakoteah proclaimed himself "Jesuee" and insisted that the only way his acolytes could reach heaven was by starving themselves to death. He threatened to kill anyone who refused to starve himself.

Eventually, Neakoteah was shot and killed by a non-acolyte. As his dead body was being washed, the Primus stove illuminating him reputedly sang a song about its flame being everlasting. . . .

An Inuk from Repulse Bay named Putjuuti also believed he was Jesus, and what better way to prove it than by baptizing his fellow Inuit? He cut a very deep wound in his scalp, and out flowed a cascade of blood. Enough to baptize his whole village.

Before Putjuuti could perform a single baptism, he died from loss of blood.

But a white man could be Jesus, too. In the 1920s, a missionary showed a picture of the bearded Jesus to some Inuit in western Hudson Bay and asked them if they knew this man. "Of course," they said. "He came here last year in a whaling ship and slept with many of our women."

Ouyerack later corrected himself, saying, "I am Jesus Christ preparing the people for when the other Jesus comes."

10

Enter Peter Sala, the best hunter, the best ice navigator, and the tallest man in the Belcher Islands. Needless to say, the other Qiqiqtarmiut treated him with great respect.

Outsiders respected Peter as well. In their 1938 expedition to the Belchers, scientists from Pittsburgh's Carnegie Museum of Natural History hired him to be their guide.

In his book *Needle to the North*, Carnegie Museum ornithologist Arthur Twomey wrote: "Ours was a dangerous sport, but Peter was an unqualified expert."

As a guide, Peter was asked to operate the expedition's outboard motorboat, although, Twomey said, "he had never in his life operated any type of machine." Even so, he learned how to operate the boat in almost no time.

The Carnegie scientists seem to have regarded Peter as a real-life Nanook of the North, and just like Nanook in Flaherty's film, he was (Twomey wrote) "seldom without a broad smile."

For the Inuit, smiling was once a survival mechanism. They often smiled when there was very little food or when a white visitor made unconscionable demands on them.

A few years later, Peter would find it impossible to smile. . . .

In the early 1930s, a new Hudson's Bay Company employee in Great Whale River had been given a bowler hat by his Scottish mother, who may have thought that such a headpiece would be necessary for Arctic survival.

The employee gave the hat to Peter, who wore it on those rare occasions when he encountered a white man. Maybe he thought this seemingly formal headpiece would bridge the gap between his culture and white man's.

On those occasions when Peter wore this hat, I can imagine the Carnegie scientists thinking of Peter not only as a real-life Nanook, but also as the local version of Charlie Chaplin.

No Charlie Chaplin film—no film of any sort—had ever been shown in the Belchers, so Peter would probably not have understood the reference if one of the Carnegie scientists had mentioned Charlie Chaplin to him.

I recently googled "Peter Sala" and learned that "There are ten professionals named Peter Sala who use LinkedIn to exchange information." As nearly as I could tell, not a single one of these professionals had the ability to navigate a boat in icy seas.

Peter sang Inuit songs when he was hunting seals in his kayak, but he also sang the occasional Christian hymn, one of which, the old woman told me, was "Nearer, My God, to Thee."

Peter probably learned such hymns from the Anglican mission in Great Whale River, where he sometimes went to retrieve the Hudson's Bay Company's supplies and mail.

Such songs might help pass the time when I'm out hunting . . . he may have thought when he heard these hymns.

After announcing that he was Jesus, Ouyerack pointed to Peter and declared that he, Peter, was God.

With his dark complexion, high cheekbones, and slightly chubby face, Peter did not resemble the storybook image of God—an elderly, woolly-whiskered Caucasian gentleman who defies the laws of gravity by sitting on a cloud.

No matter if Peter was neither Caucasian nor perched on a cloud: he was the best hunter in the Belchers.

At first Peter seemed surprised by his new identity. He took a day or two to deliberate on it, then admitted that, yes, he was in fact God.

I asked the old woman what had become of Peter's bowler hat. She shook her head. "Gone," she said.

11

In their first religious gesture, Peter and Ouyerack ordered most of the sled dogs to be killed. For those dogs were Satan. Or maybe they were just unbelievers. Either way, it was best to dispose of them.

Another reason to kill the dogs: the world was coming to an end, according to Keytowieack's Bible, and when it actually came, there would be no need to travel by dogsled . . . an Inuk could go anywhere he or she liked simply by flying through the air.

"In those days, you didn't need a boarding pass to fly," a grinning Taliriktuq told me, but his grin turned into a frown when he added, "You just needed to believe."

To newly converted Inuit in the Arctic, the notion of flying through the air had so much appeal that some of them felt obliged to cut off most of their hair. For they thought too much hair would drag them down to the earth or at least inhibit their skyward journey.

When the world ended, there would be no need to hunt seals or walrus, no need to gather berries, no need to net fish. For there would be no more hunger, Peter and Ouyerack told the other Inuit.

No more hunger—how extraordinary those words must have seemed to the Qiqiqtarmiut! No wonder they were so eager for the world to end!

The old woman had been a teenage girl at the time of the meteor shower. When I mentioned Sara, she started to cry.

The old woman's grandson had been helping me translate his grandmother's Inuktitut. "Enough for today," he told me.

Later I learned that Sara Apawkok had been one of her best friends.

On the following day, I visited the old woman again. Peter was becoming more accustomed to his new role, she told me. He informed the other Inuit that he might look the same as he looked before, but on the inside he was different. There, he was God.

Hearing this, Sara shook her head, saying, "You are Peter Sala on the outside and you are Peter Sala on the inside."

"This girl is Satan," declared Ouyerack. A Primus stove was lit and held very close to Sara's face. "Yes, she is Satan," Ouyerack repeated, gazing closely at Sara.

One of Flaherty's sons, a man named Aleck, was a believer in Peter and Ouyerack's divinity. He told Sara that he would cut off her head if she didn't change her mind. She didn't change her mind.

Aleck was Sara's half brother. He hit Sara repeatedly with a chunk of driftwood, then several others dragged her from the large snowhouse that was serving as their meeting place, and a teenage girl named Akeenik hammered away at her head with the barrel of a rifle.

Several minutes later, Akeenik returned to the snowhouse. She announced: "My hands are frozen from killing Satan. Please thaw them out for me, someone."

Sara Apawkok was probably thirteen years old at the time. Her death was just the beginning.

12

One morning I was brewing some coffee when an ATV pulled up in front of my tent. The driver was Simeonie. "I have some bad news for you," he said. "New York City is no more. Maybe America is no more, too. Come, I will show you."

On the way to Sanikiluaq, we passed a clump of Maydell's oxytropes, and Simeonie said the roots of this perennial forb tasted very good when cooked with beluga whale blubber.

"Tomorrow I will feed you this dish," Simeonie said, perhaps to make me feel better now that my country was no more.

In Sanikiluaq's small hotel, I saw a group of Inuit sitting around a TV and watching what's now referred to as 9/11. Today was September 13, so they were actually watching rebroadcast excerpts from the terrorist attack of two days earlier.

Now I realized that a Hudson Bay gale wasn't the only reason I hadn't seen any planes for the last few days: Transport Canada was following the FAA's example and grounding all its flights, including flights to the Belchers.

"So many people!" one of the Inuit remarked, pointing to the screen.

A man made a joke about New York's skyscrapers, using the Inuktitut word for penis and adding a suffix that meant giant. The others burst into laughter.

"BANG! BANG!" a woman laughed, aiming an invisible gun at the television.

My first thought was: These people are insensitive. Likewise, my second thought.

My third thought: they weren't being insensitive at all. For the world on the screen was so removed from the local world of wind and ice, rock and lichen that they could be watching a movie . . . a disaster movie or even a comedy.

One of the viewers switched channels to a Road Runner cartoon. No, protested another viewer, who switched it back. "There's an American here, and his country is falling down."

This other viewer, a man named Jacky, told me that I should drink lots of seal blood, and this would give me the strength to face the fact that my country was in trouble.

Jacky had a hole in his cheek from having been stabbed by a walrus tusk while he was hunting. Occasionally, he would reach up and feel the hole as if to make sure it was still there.

Images: the North Tower bursting into flames, a crowd of people running to escape a billowing cloud of smoke, and a substance similar to confetti floating down from the sky.

Sounds: screams, sirens, bells, bullhorns.

A two-or three-year-old boy sitting on his mother's lap pointed to the screen and laughed, "Ijur . . . na . . . ru . . . naq, ijur . . . na . . . ru . . . naq." (*Ijurnarunaq* means funny or amusing in Inuktitut.)

"Unbelievable, ladies and gentleman, just unbelievable!" exclaimed a newsman into his mike.

Unbelievable. None of the viewers seemed to know this word, so I searched my English-Inuktitut dictionary, and I couldn't find its equivalent.

Seated next to Jacky was a nephew (great-nephew?) of Aleck, the man who clubbed Sara with a piece of driftwood. He was polishing a soapstone carving (technically, serpentine) and only intermittently looking at the screen.

The North Tower burst into flames again, this time in slow motion and filmed from a different angle, and the woman with the child clapped her hands, maybe because this was a more esthetically pleasing shot of the Tower's demise than the previous one.

An attractive newswoman talking into her mike inspired these words from a woman wearing a faded Mother Hubbard dress: "Such nice clothes."

Context: we're watching a relatively small screen in a relatively small building perched atop some much-eroded, much-faulted rocks that once formed an ancient mountain range.

Simeonie rested a sympathetic hand on my shoulder and said, "Who made these attacks?" "Terrorists," I told him. "It's good that we don't get any tourists in Sanikiluaq," he said. For he did not know the word "terrorist."

Only two tourists had traveled to Sanikiluaq this year—both bird-watchers and both English.

Speaking of birds: a man walked into the hotel and showed me a soapstone carving of an eider duck. Would I like to buy it? he asked me. Maybe later, I told him.

Speaking of birds again: I noticed that one of the women looking at the TV was wearing a necklace composed artfully of bands put on Canada geese by bird banders from somewhere south of here.

More confetti. More billowing smoke. Another pretty news-woman. Aleck's nephew said he would talk to me about the 1941 murders, but only if I put away my tape recorder and used my *siut* (ears).

"How can people live so far above the ground?" asked an elder, gesturing at the city's remaining skyline.

The hotel's manager allowed me to use one of his phones to call a few friends in New York City. "We were *supposed* to have a speedy defense system," one friend said, adding, "Oh well . . . at least I'm alive."

"You are where? *Where?* You can find out about this horror show in the middle of Hudson Bay?" another asked in astonishment.

My lady friend, who lived just outside Boston, said, "America has joined the rest of the world."

There was another channel switch, not to a Road Runner cartoon but to the Reverend Billy Graham, who was saying that all of the victims of 9/11 had gone immediately to Paradise.

"*Para . . . dise!*" repeated the young boy on his mother's lap. This was perhaps his first word in English.

My ninety-one-year-old grandfather once called my mother to tell her that Billy Graham was squatting naked in his bathtub. Or maybe the squatter was Johnny Carson, he wasn't really sure.

At the time my grandfather wasn't senile, but he did watch a lot of television.

Aleck's nephew got up to leave. "Remember," he told me, pointing to one of his ears.

Most of the others got up, too. Simeonie offered to drive me back to my tent, but I said I preferred to walk. For 9/11 had affected me considerably less than the events in the Belchers of sixty years earlier, and I thought walking might help me discover why.

13

I walked past Flaherty Island's gravel pit, which—so goes the *qallu-naat* joke—is indistinguishable from the rest of the island.

In my mind, I saw the Twin Towers collapse, and on the ground I saw the waving plumes of arctic cotton (*Eriophorum angustifolium*), a sedge plant that Inuit women mix with charcoal to heal the umbilical wounds of newborns.

Floating up and down in the waves was a fleet of eider ducks speaking to each other like an orchestra of oboes.

I walked past drift logs lying askew, isolated, or piled high—the de-articulated bones of the sea.

I also walked past some washed-up coral. Contrary to what you might think, there are quite a few northern coral species, but since they don't form reef structures, they're not as blatant as tropical species.

Here was a much larger clump of Maydell's oxytropes than the one Simeonie and I had seen earlier. It was larger for a very good reason. There were several lemming burrows nearby.

Yum-m-m, says a plant's roots when it encounters the nutrient-rich home of a creature like a lemming.

In a story I heard from Markassie, two lemmings—husband and wife—envied human beings so much that they began talking like them. *You make dinner, no, you make it. To hell with you!* A snowy owl heard them shouting at each other, flew down, grabbed them, and ate them.

"That's what happens when you don't speak your own language," Markassie told me after he finished the story.

So necessary are lemmings to the diet of snowy owls that a very good lemming year means that owls will breed promiscuously, and a bad lemming year means they'll breed hardly at all.

Lemmings don't commit mass suicide by jumping off cliffs except in the Walt Disney so-called documentary, *White Wilderness*.

Another Disney moment: Walt's cameramen were trying to shoot (film) a pair of polar bear cubs, but the mother bear kept interfering, often aggressively, so the cameramen shot (killed) the mother in order to shoot (film) the cubs.

"Disney is one of the great liquidators of Western culture," observed Czech artist-animator Jan Švankmajer.

A few years earlier, in Igloolik, Nunavut, an Inuit elder was telling me a story about the origin of the earth while his grandchildren were watching *Creepshow 2* on television. Occasionally, the man would look at the screen. Then he looked at it more often. Finally, he fixed his gaze on it . . .

. . . and I never did find out how the earth originated.

The giant hypnotic eye of a television screen—almost *any* screen—demands that viewers stare at it rather than, as Odysseus's men did with the giant eye of the Cyclops in *The Odyssey,* thrust a spear into it.

"It's life I believe in, not machines," wrote ecologist Loren Eiseley.

Kalopaling *with victim*

I saw another fleet of eider ducks, but I didn't see a *kalopaling,* a giant eider duck or a giant dressed in clothes made of eider duck skins, opinions disagree. A *kalopaling*'s specialty: dragging people into the sea, drowning them, and then eating them.

Several scaber-stalked *Leecinum* mushrooms looked positively robust compared to the ground-hugging, wind-snipped plants around them. You can huff, and you can puff, but you can't blow us down, they seemed to be saying to the wind.

In his popular book *Kabloona*, French writer Gontran de Poncsins referred to the Arctic tundra as "a dead earth almost colorless in its brown monotony." The bright orange *Leecinum* caps proved Monsieur de Poncsins wrong.

In the fall, the flaming scarlet of bearberry leaves and the golden glow of dwarf willow leaves also prove him wrong.

The word "tundra" is derived from the Finnish word *tunturi*, which means treeless hills. But most tundras do have trees, albeit trees of a dwarf variety whose anchoring roots protect them against strong winds. Like the aforementioned dwarf willows, which I found almost impossible not to step on.

The gale was dying down. Instead of a single raven, there were now four or five ravens making fanciful pirouettes in the air above my tent. I shouted at them: *"Ijurnarunaq, ijuranarunaq!"*

Beside my tent, a late-blooming Arctic poppy was cheerfully lifting its gold-yellow blossoms to the sky.

At last I realized why I was more affected by the events of sixty years ago in the Belcher Islands than by the terrorist attack on New York City of two days ago—there was no mediation, none whatsoever, between me and the old woman's eyes.

"Only connect," wrote novelist E. M. Forster.

14

From my notebook: A bright Sunday morning, and almost every person of sound mind and body seems to be out berry-picking rather than attending Sanikiluaq's igloo-shaped church. A very good sign . . .

If, according to Anglican missionaries, sewing on Sunday offends Jesus, then berry-picking on Sunday doubtless would be even more offensive to him.

The Bible was even more strict than the missionaries. Exodus 35:2 states that "whosoever doeth work therein [on the Sabbath] shall be put to death."

"Satan" was the word used repeatedly by early missionaries to remind the Inuit of their great adversary. Satan was all around them, in every tundra nook and cranny, those missionaries said.

The missionaries extolled the virtues of the Holy Land, saying it was Satan-free. In the 1920s, an Inuk in eastern Hudson Bay was so inspired by this news that he slid into his kayak and began paddling toward the Holy Land. He was never heard from again.

Satan still has a strong presence in the Arctic. One thousand-year-old petroglyphs with incised shamanic faces occupy rocks on Qajartalik Island in Hudson Strait. The local Inuit, who are Pentecostal Baptists, call these faces "Devil Masks" and periodically try to etch crosses onto them.

The Qiqiqtarmiut assumed Satan was a real person . . . as did a beaming Jehovah's Witness I recently met in Boston. He informed me that Satan might be my next door neighbor, my banker, or even a member of my family.

At forty-seven, Keytowieack—the Bible reader—would have been considered an elder. For the Inuit, elders were regarded as fonts of wisdom, so Keytowieack probably figured that the other Inuit would listen to him when he said that Peter Sala and Ouyerack were not God and Jesus, respectively.

But the growing hysteria eliminated any possible wisdom he might have imparted. A hysteria Peter Sala's mother fanned by screaming that Keytowieack was Satan. "Satan! Satan! Satan!" several others yelled, pointing at him.

Peter himself had this terse dialogue with Keytowieack: "You are Satan." "I'm not Satan." "I am God, and I say you are Satan." "There is only one God, and he is not here in this snowhouse."

Once he heard this denial of his status as God, Peter yanked loose a slat from a sleeping platform in the snowhouse and flung it at Keytowieack. "I have hit Satan in the mouth!" he announced.

A bleeding Keytowieack retreated to his own snowhouse and opened his Bible. Maybe he wanted to find a passage that would explain the behavior of his fellow Inuit . . . or maybe just a passage that would offer him solace in what was rapidly becoming a desperate situation.

Keytowieack was asleep when the old woman, then a teenage girl, peered into his snowhouse. It was at this time that she saw the pages of his Bible "moving like grass moves in a strong wind."

The snowhouse had no opening where even a gentle wind could have entered, the old woman added.

The next day Peter, with a harpoon in each hand, kicked down the wall of Keytowieack's snowhouse. He threw one of the harpoons at Keytowieack, pinning him to the ground.

"Look at me, for I am God," Peter said. Keytowieack did not look at him. Peter repeated his words. Keytowieack looked the other way.

A man named Adlaytok joined Peter. "I have borrowed some bullets from Jesus," he said, by which he meant Ouyerack. Peter gestured toward Keytowieack, and Adlaytok shot him twice, then kicked him.

Peter thrust his other harpoon into Keytowieack's face, after which he shouted, "I have killed Satan!"

"Everyone was thinking, 'I'm going to be the next Satan,'" Simeonie said. And the old woman told me: "Parents told their children to agree with everything Peter and Ouyerack said . . . even if they said that *qallunaat* had six legs!"

On the evening of the non-churchgoing Sunday, many of the Qiqiqtarmiut had red lips and red teeth . . . not because they were victims of religious violence, but because they'd been eating the berries they had picked.

15

From my notebook: Flakes of snow locked together in weightless spokes flutter around crazily and melt when they touch the ground. The silence is so complete that it brings a slight whistling to my ears. A lovely evening. So lovely, in fact, that all thoughts of 9/11 have been jettisoned from my mind.

The silence brings a slight whistling to my ears. I liked that sentence so much that I included it in a letter to Farley Mowat, who had asked me to send him some sort of message from the Belchers, one of the few places in the Canadian North he'd never visited.

Paper offers a physical landscape, with four separate directions— north, south, east, and west. You can crumple it, spill coffee on it, and create abstract art on it with arrows and cross outs.

You can even use paper for your lavatorial needs—don't try doing that with your computer. . . .

Imagine that you've just gotten a fervently scrawled letter from your friend Mushpan Mike in Last Chance, Alaska, telling you that he's fallen in love with a female moose. Then imagine getting the same letter as an email. It's no longer love.

Since cursive writing is not taught anymore in schools, you can say good-bye to fervently scrawled letters from Mushpan Mike.

First sentence of a recent article in *The Wall Street Journal* describing new pens: "Trying to write a note by hand after years of typing on a keyboard or a smartphone can be discouraging."

In the same issue of *The Wall Street Journal,* an advertisement shows a giant hand reaching out to touch an up-to-date smartphone like Michelangelo's God bringing life to Adam. The caption reads: Touching is believing.

Digital technology = the latest religion?

As God, Peter Sala did not touch—instead, he harpooned. That he seldom missed his target when he was hunting seals or walrus must have enforced his divinity. . . .

I asked Markassie whether he remembered the murders. He shook his head. He was only a year old at the time. Also, his family was camped in a different part of Flaherty Island, and "we only knew what was happening in our own camp and nowhere else in the world."

Ernie Riddell, the local Hudson's Bay Company trader, was located on neighboring Tukarak Island, and he didn't know about the murders, either. Nor did the Royal Canadian Mounted Police.

Over twenty years earlier, in their only visit to the Belchers, the Mounties had examined two separate instances where deranged individuals had threatened to go on a killing spree. Those individuals were killed by other Qiqiqtarmiut before they could engage in those sprees.

The Mounties did not prosecute the killers of the would-be killers because they were ignorant of the law. Or ignorant of white man's law. The Qiqitarmiut had their own time-honored ways of dealing with violent misfits.

Or they knew how to deal with such misfits before the arrival of an alien religion. . . .

The visiting Mounties recommended that a permanent RCMP detachment be established on the Belchers. An idle recommendation, for the Canadian government refused to fund such a remote posting.

Now it was Markassie's turn to ask me a question. He said, "I keep hearing about this word in English called 'Internet.' What does it mean? When I first heard it, I thought it was the same as *initait* [a drying rack], but I now think it means something else. . . ."

Might we consider a person like Markassie "pre-Internet," just as we might have considered his not-so-distant ancestors pre-Contact?

I told Markassie to imagine a spiderweb so enormous that it encompasses the wide, wide world. I did not mention the spider's prey, however.

16

In February of 1941, the Inuit in Peter and Ouyerack's camp moved to Tukurak Island, where they hoped the hunting might be better than on Flaherty Island. They brought their new religion with them.

Ouyerack was talking increasingly about the end of the world. He did not think this was such a bad thing, except for those who did not believe in it. They should be killed, he said, unless they were good hunters.

The Flaherty Islanders were now in the camp of a man named Qarak, who, according to Arthur Twomey, was "the Tukarak symbol of justice, but . . . justice that was strong and violent."

The other Qiqiqtarmiut referred to Qarak as "Big Mouth."

Rumor has it that whenever Qarak sneezed, he would beat up his wife because he thought she was responsible for giving him the sneeze.

In the same camp lived Ikpak, the twenty-six-year old son of the recently murdered Keytowieack. He may or may not have been aware of his father's death, but he shared his father's opinion of Ouyerack—namely, that he was not Jesus Christ.

Ikpak's wife, Eva, warned him to keep his thoughts to himself, but he didn't listen to her. He approached Ouyerack, then said, "You are not Jesus Christ, and the world is not coming to an end." Dangerous words!

But the end of the world—the natural world—may not be far away now. By a recent reckoning of the International Union for Conservation of Nature, 30 to 50 percent of all flora and fauna could be extinct by the middle of our own century.

And not just readily visible organisms will be gone. With the melting of sea ice in the Arctic and the Antarctic, thousands of never-to-be-documented microorganisms will go extinct or have already gone extinct.

"If we don't stabilize our rapidly declining ecosystems, then the planet will come to look like a spaceship run by technical geniuses," wrote biologist-conservationist E. O. Wilson.

To find the location of Qarak's camp, I googled a map of Tukarak Island. At the top of my screen was an advertisement for National Car Rental, although no car, rental or otherwise, has ever been driven on roadless Tukarak Island.

Ouyerack may have been short, but he was not a garden gnome. Even so, my computer inexplicably decided to route me to a garden gnome website while I was trying to get online information about Ouyerack's activities in Qarak's camp on Tukurak Island.

Speculation: the raised basaltic reef that constitutes Tukarak Island has never known the presence of a single garden gnome.

Specifically, the website was designed for people who like to purchase garden gnomes, stab them in the head with a knife, and then post online photos of them in this sorry condition on the site.

"Man, your head is haunted," wrote the nineteenth-century philosopher Max Stirner in *The Ego and Its Own*.

Gazing at the garden gnomes with knives protruding from their heads, I had the following thought: Better tango rhythms than algorithms!

17

Qarak's camp on Tukurak Island was only a short distance from Laddie Harbour, where the rotting remains of Flaherty's boat still rested, and even closer to Flaherty's overwintering camp on the island.

Qarak was old enough to have met Flaherty: might the filmmaker have given him "gun food" (popcorn)?

Whether or not Qarak had partaken of Flaherty's gun food, he did like guns. "My father told me that Qarak was always threatening people with his rifle," one of my informants told me.

Ouyerack was not pleased that Ikpak had denied his divinity. He said to Qarak: "Jesus will be coming soon, and he will not want to meet people like Ikpak."

He did not need to say another word. Grabbing his rifle, Qarak shot Ikpak twice between the shoulder blades, and when he noticed his victim was still moving, he put a bullet in Ikpak's head.

"Satan is dead!" announced Ouyerack. Again. Then he pointed to the halo around his head. Might this putative halo have been a vestige of the traditional Inuit belief that *angakut* are bathed in a perpetually bright light?

Inuit *angakut* reputedly knew *irinaliutit*, or magic words. Ouyerack seemed to know only one magic word—Satan—but that turned out to be enough.

Perhaps because her own life might have been at risk, Eva accepted the loss of her husband, saying, "He was a bad man—he was Satan."

Qarak was Eva's father. He seems not to have been perturbed that he killed his own son-in-law. Quite the contrary. "We will sleep well tonight, for I have killed Satan," Qarak told the other Inuit in his camp.

Peter Sala returned from an unsuccessful hunting expedition. Right away he said Ikpak's body should be placed in a cairn, but Qarak did not think Satan deserved a proper burial.

"*I am God*," Peter threatened, and Qarak backed down. Ikpak was placed under a pile of rocks.

As God, Peter was not exactly love, but he did appear to be mellowing: the bodies of Keytowieack and Sara had not been given any sort of burial.

The Inuit usually buried their dead in cairns of neatly piled rocks. One day I visited the cairn on the hill above my tent and looked at the skeleton inside it. The skull boasted a wide grin that seemed to say, How glad I am to have lived and died before the arrival of white man's religion. . . .

18

F*rom my notebook*: Today's temperature is several degrees below freezing, with (mirabile dictu!) no wind, and the air has a sharp high latitude clarity that I wouldn't exchange for any other air in the world.

For our species, the word "cold" invariably means something bad: cold feet, a cold stare, a cold shoulder, and the cold that kills cell phone battery life. Which would you prefer, a date with a coldie or a date with a hottie?

By popular demand, hot—courtesy of climate change—is winning over cold virtually everywhere in the world. And by popular demand, today's weather exists primarily on a screen, conveyed either via a forecaster or an app.

Several years ago, on a Boston street, a woman gazing at her digital device walked directly into me. "Sorry," she apologized, "I was just trying to find out the weather."

Last winter my lady friend and I paraded up and down that same Boston street wearing full-body mosquito nets. Winter is not the usual time for mosquitoes, but no one seemed to notice our unusual garb. They were too busy gazing at their iDevices.

Not so long ago, if you didn't pay attention to the world around you, you might end up being eaten, but now alas! our species has rendered extinct almost all of the creatures that once had a taste for human flesh.

One consequence of inhabiting a world without predators: a dulling of the eyes.

Could the current zombie craze be a subliminal desire on the part of our species to restore the balance of nature by creating a predator, albeit a mostly dead one, that likes to dine on our meat?

And could the seemingly mindless saunter of iDevice users perhaps be contributing to that craze?

Such saunterers commonly walk into lampposts or garbage cans while texting, tumble into manholes while talking on their cell phones, or smash into other people while trying to find out about (among other things) the weather.

One of the few surviving predators is the polar bear. In the Belchers, polar bears were once common, but with the near-vanishing of sea ice, their numbers have decreased significantly.

A bear is always listening for the crunch of its prey's skull, Simeonie told me. After hearing that crunch, it can dine at its leisure on the brain and then on various fleshy body parts, without interference from pesky arms or legs.

The human brain itself has considerable appeal for bears. After all, our brains are mostly composed of fats (specifically, myelin-coated dendrites), and eating fats is necessary if you . . . or a bear . . . wants to survive in the Arctic.

If the bear doesn't hear a telltale crunch when it clamps down its jaws, it'll usually wander off in search of other prey, Simeonie told me, adding that the Qiqiqtarmiut used to wear thick fur hats to diminish the possibility of a crunching sound.

In the winter of 2013, there were twenty deaths from polar bears in the Belchers. The victims happened not to be Inuit, but beluga whales that had become trapped in the ice.

So there I was, writing up these notes inside my tent, when all of a sudden I heard a sharp scratching sound on the tent's fabric. My first thought was: *polar bear!*

My visitor turned out to be the Inuk who tried to sell me the eider duck carving while I was watching 9/11. In his hand was a different, more self-possessed eider duck than the previous one.

A one-two punch of climate change and hydroelectric dams on the mainland has affected both the sea ice and the sea's salinity in this part of Hudson Bay, with the result that the eider duck population has gone into decline . . .

. . . but the bird in the Inuk's hand seemed to be thumbing its beak at the sufferings the formerly natural world was flinging its way.

"This bird I carved, he was in the stone already," the man informed me. "I just liberated him."

I bought the carving for $50, a cheap price for such a magical creation.

19

Peter Sala's readings of ice conditions made him a valuable guide for Ernie Riddell, who hired Peter several times a year to take him to the Hudson's Bay Company post at Great Whale River so he could retrieve mail and get trade items for his Tukarak Island store.

On March 12, 1941, Ernie and Peter set off on the three-day dog-sled journey over the ice to Great Whale. Sharp winds stabbed their faces and dusted their eyebrows with ice.

Peter was such an expert handler of dogs that Robert Flaherty reputedly filmed him as a teenage dog team driver in his lost Belcher footage.

It might seem strange that a person who knew so much about sled dogs might think they were Satan . . .

. . . unless you remember that what's on the outside of a creature, whether a dog or a human being, isn't always the same as what's on the inside.

By 2001, sled dogs had mostly been replaced by snowmobiles in the Belchers. A snowmobile might be more efficient, Markassie told me, "but you can't eat it if you get stuck somewhere."

A few years later, in Inukjuak, I learned that SFU is the Inuit texting acronym for "snowmobile fucked up," and that POOS is the acronym for "passed out on snowmobile." Passed out either from drinking too much or from a drug overdose.

On the same visit to Inukjuak, I saw a woman texting while breastfeeding an infant. Will that infant grow up associating screens with nurture?

As for myself, I associate coffee with nurture, and I was grinding a bag of robusta in Sanikiluaq's Northern Store when Jacky—the Inuk with the hole in his cheek—walked up to me.

"That attack on your country," Jacky told me. "I don't believe it happened. I think it was made up for TV."

In the store's DVD bin, I noticed *The Towering Inferno*. If Jacky had seen it, then this disaster movie about a fire that breaks out in a state-of-the-art high rise in San Francisco might explain why he thought 9/11 was a fiction.

At the time of my visit, the highest structure in the Belchers was only two stories high—hardly towering at all. This might be another reason Jacky regarded 9/11 as a fiction: buildings as high as the World Trade Center could not exist except on a screen.

20

During the trip to Great Whale River, Peter Sala kept repeating, "I am a bad man. . . ." He did not elaborate.

As soon as Peter and Ernie arrived in Great Whale, Peter went to see Harold Udgarten, who had met Robert Flaherty in 1914 and who was still working for the Hudson's Bay Company twenty-seven years later.

Many of the Hudson Bay Inuit, including Peter himself, referred to Harold as "our white brother," although Harold was actually of mixed blood—part Norwegian and part Cree.

All of a sudden Harold burst into the room where Ernie was chatting with another Hudson's Bay Company employee. "Have you heard about the recent murders in the Belchers?" he said to Ernie.

During his long tenure with the Hudson's Bay Company, "Old Harold," as he was now called, had developed a reputation for protecting the Inuit from the not always pleasant demands of *qallunaat,* which was probably why Peter chose to tell him rather than Ernie about the murders.

I wondered whether Peter had implicated himself during his visit to Harold. "I'll find out for you," said a Cyberian friend to whom I had told the story of the Belcher murders. He spent close to two hours with his computer . . . to no avail.

Two hours seemed to me a long time, but the Cyberian admitted that he got a surge of adrenaline every time he successfully down-loaded something, and the longer he worked at it, the more potent the surge.

Confession: I get a surge of adrenaline every time I upload myself—i.e., get up and walk away from my computer.

"Our inventions are wont to be pretty toys," wrote Thoreau. "They are but improved means to an unimproved end."

I asked another friend who happened to be a psychic rather than a Cyberian to call up the spirit of Thoreau and ask him (it?) what he thought of computers, so she went into a trance. The spirit's response was, "All the folks in the afterlife use them except me."

Until the end of his life, Ernie Riddell couldn't get Harold's voice "asking that question" out of his head.

Telegraph message from the HBC store in Great Whale River to the Company's headquarters in Winnipeg on March 14, 1941:

HAVE RECEIVED INFORMATION THAT THREE MURDERS
HAVE BEEN COMMITTED RECENTLY IN BELCHERS. ADVISE
IMMEDIATE POLICE INVESTIGATION.

21

From my notebook: Sea seething with high chop and spume. Tent blown down by the wind for a final time. Relocated to the hotel. Broken TV in room. Manager says he'll give me a room where the TV works. No, I protested, I like my TVs broken.

I visited "Siut" and, as per his earlier request, brought my ears rather than my tape recorder with me.

"You asked about those murders," Siut told me. "I am a cousin to Ouyerack, and I am a cousin to Keytowieack, so their blood is in me, and I feel bad for all of them."

"We are Inuit, so we share," added Siut's wife.

Siut's wife gave me the following piece of information: Ouyerack's father had been murdered when he, Ouyerack, was a young boy, and this might have made him want to become a murderer himself.

Siut himself visited Tukarak Island to get soapstone for his carvings. He told me that the soapstone on Tukarak sometimes turned blood-red because it had been a witness to Ikpak's murder.

Siut gave me a greenish (not blood-red!) soapstone carving of a polar bear. "It's for you . . . because of what happened to your country," he said.

The carving was a gift, but it also carried a message that said "It's time to talk about a less painful subject." So we now talked about the Toronto Blue Jays and what a lousy season they'd had. A far less painful subject.

I gave Sanikiluaq a gift of my own—a lecture about Arctic plant ecology in the village school. During this lecture, I often had to shout so my voice could be heard above the shrieking wind. A common problem here, one of the teachers told me.

I told the audience that climate change was bringing many vascular plants from temperate regions to the North, with the result that local lichens will likely die off because they won't be able to compete with the southern invaders . . .

"Just like what the *qallunaat* have been doing to us," an Inuk in the audience remarked, to a mixture of laughter and applause.

. . . and that since lichens contribute significant amounts of nitrogen to the nitrogen-deprived soil of the North, the loss of those lichens could have a disastrous effect on local ecology.

I also mentioned the high latitude/high altitude plant called *Diapensia*, sometimes referred to as the "cushion plant" because it grows close to the ground in a mosslike mat. Its dead leaves remain on the plant through the winter, sheltering it from the snow and from wind abrasion.

Long live death, I was getting ready to say, but then I saw several elders in the audience who'd given me stories about the 1941 killings, and I held my tongue.

Question from the audience: "How can you be a *Naaqtuuq* when your stomach is a normal size?" *Naaqtuuq*, one of several Inuit names for white man, means "Big Belly."

A woman in the audience raised her hand. "*Diapensia* is the first flower to bloom in the spring here," she remarked, then said: "I feel the land is smiling when I see its flowers." She was smiling herself.

The wind was not smiling, though. It suddenly blew open a window behind me and then made a loud caterwauling scream, as if to protest its exclusion from the evening's event.

22

After my lecture, one of the teachers took me to a room in the school where I could check my emails. Seated at one of the computers was a twelve- or thirteen-year-old girl. She was playing a video game that featured Godzilla-type monsters and did not seem to notice me.

If the medium is the message, then there's no difference between playing a monster video game and googling Harold Udgarten.

A popular misconception about evolution—it progresses for the good of a species.

Another misconception about evolution—it occurs only over a long time.

Just as numerous birds have gone in a single generation from being feeders in the wild to feeders in garbage dumps, so *Homo sapiens* has evolved in slightly less than a generation from being more or less a free-ranging species to being a species that's permanently tethered to a screen.

In his book *Exodus to the Virtual World,* Edward Castronova writes that the greatest migration in human history is the current move from the real to the virtual world.

I now joined this migration myself.

"We've gotten color-coded terrorist alerts," a friend emailed me. "When you get back, you'll see surveillance screens all over the place," another emailer wrote. A third wrote: "My life will be changed forever when I buy Apple's new iPod. . . ."

A fourth emailer made this not necessarily funny joke: "If you eat the seals and walruses there, you'll become a belcher yourself."

While I was responding to my emails, I had this thought: I could be a *kalopaling* (giant man-eating eider duck) typing these words, and no one would be aware of the fact.

And how did I know that one of my correspondents wasn't a *kalopaling*?

Email from one *kalopaling* to another: "Social media are awesome, dude. I meet so many human beings, and not a single one of them realizes that I'm going to eat him/her."

Markassie had agreed to take me to Camsell Island. But I didn't tell any of my e-correspondents that I would soon be visiting this obscure chunk of granite south of Tukarak Island. I would tell them in person when I got home.

23

F*rom my notebook:* Fog-ridden day. Both land and sea appear
swathed in moist cotton. Markassie navigates by studying
qimugjuit—snow formations sculpted by the prevailing wind. Also
by using his time-honored sense of direction. And, occasionally,
by tasting the seawater.

"I don't need a GPS," Markassie informed me shortly after we set
off. "That's because I already know where I am."

The Inuit have (had?) enlarged hippocampuses because they need
(needed?) complex mental maps of their surroundings. This loss of
such maps is starting to have dire consequences. . . .

In 2013, I heard about a seal hunter in East Greenland whose boat
was found miles from his intended destination. The dead man was
still holding his GPS. Apparently, its receiver had failed.

I also heard about an Inuk with a GPS-equipped snowmobile who
smashed into a large boulder on Baffin Island. The boulder wrecked

his snowmobile, along with his GPS. He was only a few miles from his village, but he began walking in the wrong direction and nearly froze to death.

In case of a polar bear attack, Markassie had brought along a high-powered rifle, although he hadn't seen many polar bears the last few years. "The earth is getting too warm for them," he said.

The word in Inuktitut for climate change is *uggianaqtuq*, which means "a friend acting strangely."

Even without climate change, the cold calculus of lower Hudson Bay leaves very little margin for error by polar bears, an animal much more adapted to higher latitudes.

Another strike against polar bears: with climate change, they've recently been mating with grizzlies. The hybridized offspring (pizzly bears?) will have much greater difficulty surviving the rigors of the North than they would if their parents shared the same genes.

In the boat, I studied Markassie's face. It resembled the contour lines on a topographic map, and when he grinned, impressive new lines would appear. He grinned when he pointed to something too far away for me to see.

Anthropologist Claude Levi-Strauss was astonished that Indian tribes in the Amazon could see the planet Venus in broad daylight. They were astonished that he couldn't.

Whether in the Amazon or in the Arctic, those who have good observational skills are more likely to survive than those who don't.

Camsell Island, a low flat rock a mile or so in diameter, was named for Canadian geologist Charles Camsell, who never visited it.

After we landed on the island, I could now see the object Markassie had pointed to—a lone pampers stuck (or frozen?) to the rocks several feet above the high tide mark.

A *pampers*—from where might Hudson Bay's notoriously whimsical currents have brought it?

Except for the marooned pampers, the island did not seem to have any evidence of visits by human beings—not even the fifty-five-gallon oil drums, shotgun shells, candy bar wrappers, or empty potato chip bags that litter most parts of the Arctic.

We were in a harbor surrounded by snow-draped, fog-encompassed geology. "Here," Markassie said. "It happened here. . . ."

24

Mina, Peter Sala's twenty-five-year-old sister, must have liked the idea of having Jesus Christ as her boyfriend, because she left her husband, a man named Mosee, and went to live in Ouyerack's snowhouse after she learned he was Jesus.

"First Mina was normal, then she was crazy," the old woman told me.

On March 29, 1941 the harbor was covered with thick ice. The outside temperature would have been quite a few degrees below zero. Not a temperature that even an Inuk would want to experience without the proper garments.

All at once Mina began running from snowhouse to snowhouse, shouting that the world was coming to an end, and that Jesus would soon be arriving to take the Qiqiqtarmiut to a better place than the Belcher Islands.

"We must go out on the ice to meet our Saviour," Mina proclaimed. "Why can't Jesus meet us in our snowhouses?" someone asked. "Because that is not his way," she replied.

I recently googled "Mina Sala," and my first hit took me to a grand boutique hotel called Mina A'Salaam in Dubai.

A stout, powerful woman, Mina started pushing people onto the ice and then lashing at them with a dog whip. Especially, she lashed at other women and small children. All the while she was dancing like a dervish and shouting, "Come, Jesus, come!"

An Inuit dog whip has a sealskin lash that's flung forward and back with a quick turn of the wrist. When it strikes, it has a report like a pistol. Lashed dogs often can be seen missing an eye or an ear.

Farther and farther onto the ice Mina whipped her victims, telling them that Jesus would soon be kayaking down from the sky.

Jesus paddling a kayak—no one seemed to question this. Or to question the notion of Jesus paddling it vertically.

According to one of my informants, Mina's sister Kumudluk helped her force people onto the ice, but then she (the sister) realized that this was not a good thing to do and went back to the shore . . . by herself.

All of a sudden Mina shouted, "Naked we must meet our Saviour!" Then she rushed toward the other Qiqiqtarmiut and began ripping off their clothes and pulling off their *kamiks* (boots).

She even tore the clothes off her own elderly mother.

81

Perhaps because Jesus would soon be kayaking down from the sky, no one offered Mina any resistance.

Ouyerack was hunting on the other side of the island. If he had been in the camp, would he have stopped Mina? Maybe, but maybe not. For he might have been Jesus, but he was also waiting for Jesus himself.

"Wow! This would make a terrific movie!" a Cyberian friend said when I told her about Mina forcing people onto the ice. "Of course, the ending would have to be changed. . . ."

Question: Why a movie? Why not, for instance, a book? Or even a lecture?

Answer: Because it usually requires less thought to watch a movie than to read a book or listen to a lecture, and facility has become the ultimate goal of our species.

When facility is the highest of all values, sitting and watching a screen becomes the defining activity. Or lack of activity.

"Virtue rejects facility to be her companion," wrote French philosopher Michel de Montaigne, adding: "She requires a craggy, rough, and thorny way."

Fat flakes of snow were now fluttering down from the sky like the slow emptying of a celestial bin.

In the distance, I heard a high-pitched keening that sounded like a musical rendition of the island's history. The wind was picking up. Markassie shot me a glance whose message was clear: Let's leave soon, or we might be stuck here for a long time. . . .

I quickly envisioned the scene: Mina struggling to get the clothes off first one, then another person. Parkas, sealskin trousers, and *kamiks* scattered about the ice. The dog whip snapping. Children crying. Breaths forming large balloons in the cold air.

And everyone naked except Mina, who had decided to greet her Savior fully clothed.

"Some people say they've heard the ghosts of children here," Markassie shouted into the wind.

It was probably the cold that brought several of the adults back to their senses. Mina's husband Mosee and Peter Sala's wife, Anowtelik, each grabbed a child and headed back to the shore, then grabbed another child, and another.

"Help me with the children," Anowtelik yelled at Mina, "or they will freeze." "It doesn't matter if they freeze," Mina replied. "The world will soon be coming to an end, and then they will be fine."

Each of the six people who froze to death was related to Peter Sala: his son, his adopted son, his widowed sister, two of his nephews, and his mother.

However terrible the circumstance, Inuit men almost never cry, but when Peter heard about the deaths of his family members on the ice of Camsell Island, he began sobbing.

Needless to say, Jesus did not show up on Camsell Island on that cold March day in 1941.

Author seated on *komatik* (dogsled) *(courtesy of the author)*

Typical East Greenland village scene *(courtesy of the author)*

Female and male eider duck *(courtesy of the author)*

Belcher women processing eider down in the traditional way *(courtesy of the author)*

Nanook of the North listens to the voices inside a record player (*courtesy of the author*)

Nanook of the North throwing a spear (*courtesy of unknown 1920s magazine*)

Filmmaker Robert Flaherty
(courtesy of unknown 1920s magazine)

Ninety-three-year-old Johnny Inukpuk, cousin of "Nanook" *(courtesy of the author)*

Peter Sala (on left), with two unidentified Inuit
(courtesy of the Avataq Cultural Institute)

Peter Sala with an unknown woman
(courtesy of the Avataq Cultural Institute)

The grave of Peter Sala
(courtesy of the author)

Mina in Port Harrison, 1948
(*courtesy of the Avataq Cultural Institute*)

Grave marker in Moose Factory
cemetery (*courtesy of the author*)

ATVs, not Suburus,
roam the Belcher
Islands (*courtesy of the
author*)

Idling walrus *(courtesy of the author)*

The view from the author's tent, with walrus bones in the foreground. *(courtesy of the author)*

Burial cairn above the author's tent (*courtesy of the author*)

The author listening to an *Umbilicaria* lichen (*courtesy of Tom Murray*)

25

As Markassie and I were pushing his boat into the water, I noticed (unbelievable!) a battered-looking laptop perched on the rocks directly above me.

A marooned pampers is one thing, but a marooned laptop is another: How could it have ended up at such a seemingly improbable place as this?

Optimistic thought: Some Inuit kid must have thrown away the laptop when he/she realized how it was affecting his/her life.

Instead of giving kids computers and conditioning them to be little robots, parents should give their kids hand lenses and tell them to dig up the playground, proclaimed Canadian environmental activist David Suzuki.

Evolutionary theory explains that every species is related to every other species, which is doubtless the reason children connect so readily with other organisms. *Look, Mommy! A cute little earthworm!*

Or once connected with other organisms. Most organisms kids tend to observe nowadays are virtual, offered to them by screens. *Look, Mommy! A cute little stegosaurus-E.T. hybrid!*

On the virtual versus the actual: I recently told a friend's seven-year-old daughter that Siri, Apple's beloved voice-activated digital assistant, had died in a car crash ("She was texting while driving," I said), and the girl burst into tears. "She didn't cry this hard when her grandmother died," her mother told me.

As we were heading back to Sanikiluaq, Markassie raised his voice above the wind: "A few years ago, a German went to Camsell to study the rocks, and I think he threw away that *pinnguaq* [plaything] because it stopped working. . . ."

By *pinnguaq*, he meant the marooned laptop.

Later I heard that the German geologist didn't leave his malfunctioning laptop on the island, but brought it back to Sanikiluaq and tried to get it fixed there. Not surprisingly, there were no computer repair shops in the village.

So how did the laptop reach Camsell Island? Left by a non-German scientist? Dropped out of a plane? Somehow washed ashore? Or perhaps deposited there by Amaguq, the Inuit trickster god? I never found out. . . .

On the trip back to Sanikiluaq, a sudden gust of wind blew off my woolen toque. In one deft movement, Markassie reached out and grabbed it before it could touch the sea. "I've done that many times before," he grinned.

Once again Markassie saw something that I didn't—not a pampers this time, but Sanikiluaq's igloo-shaped church. The wind had blown away every last shred of fog, and in the distance, the church looked like a white marble.

26

Ernie Riddell and Peter Sala returned to the Belchers on April 2, 1941. When Ernie learned about the deaths on Camsell Island, he quickly sent the following telegram message to the Royal Canadian Mounted Police:

THERE HAVE BEEN FURTHER MURDERS COME IMMEDIATELY.

Near his post on Tukarak Island, Ernie marked out a landing strip with coal sacks, then started waiting for a police plane to show up.

"I don't think we're safe," Ernie's clerk Lou Bradbury said.

After a google of "Lou Bradbury + Hudson's Bay Company" produced no useful results, Google had a question for me: might I be interested in "Mary Lou Bradbury?"

Ernie took a .22 rifle with him wherever he went. One day he went fishing and returned to his post with a bucket of arctic char. The

Inuit who saw him must have thought: What a strange man—he hunts fish with a rifle.

Stuck for millennia in Tukarak Island's landlocked ponds, the arctic char have developed giant heads, tumorlike humps on their snouts, and prognathous lower jaws. Even so, they're still good to eat.

Stay tuned for some thoughts on the no less peculiar morphologies of future *Homo sapiens*. . . .

The Anglican minister in Great Whale River, the Rev. George Neilsen, had accompanied Ernie and Peter on their dogsled trip back to the Belchers. For the Rev. Neilsen wanted to "help the Eskimoes with their spiritual difficulties."

On helping "Eskimoes" with their spiritual difficulties: In the Central Canadian Arctic, an Anglican missionary had been repeatedly telling the local Inuit that Man was the most beautiful thing God ever created. So what's the most beautiful thing God created? he asked an Inuk. Caribou! the elder exclaimed.

Upon hearing the word "caribou" rather than "Man," the irate missionary smacked the elder with a Bible, which proves that the Good Book, so-called, has a certain clout. . . .

On the Bible's clout: More than a quarter of all Americans think the Bible predicted 9/11.

The Reverend Jerry Falwell and Pat Buchanan regarded 9/11 as a divine judgment on a society that tolerates homosexuality and abortion. Would they have called the Belcher killings a divine judgement on a society that believes plants, driftwood, rocks, and even shit have souls?

Question: Why are there plenty of televangelists in America, but not a single tele-ecologist?

On a nature walk I once led outside Boston, I turned over a log and pointed to a red-backed salamander. "What kind of worm is that?" asked a high school science teacher.

During the same walk, we found a small plant called a sundew, or *Drosera*. A man suddenly backed away with a fearful look on his face when I mentioned that the plant was carnivorous. I soon realized that he wasn't trying to be funny.

Note: The trichomes on a sundew secrete enzymes that trap insects rather than human beings, for our size makes us culinarily uninteresting.

Once the Greek hero Antaeus lost physical contact with the earth, he was lifted into the air and crushed to death by the he-man (some would say moron) Hercules.

"God will protect us," the Rev. Neilsen told Ernie and Lou Bradbury, then gave them some of his oatmeal molasses cookies, which, along with the Anglican faith, he dispensed wherever he went.

27

The killings in the Belchers happened at a time when the word "remote" meant something other than a car starter, computer mouse, channel changer, or desktop manager, so the RCMP couldn't investigate those killings then as quickly as they could today.

Another reason for the Mounties' slow response: the killings occurred at the beginning of World War II, and every available plane had been requisitioned by the Royal Canadian Air Force for use in Europe.

Next to the carnage in Europe, nine deaths on some remote islands in Hudson Bay might seem like a very small number, but "the apothecium [the place where the spores are made] of a lichen [can seem] disproportionately large compared with the universe," wrote Thoreau.

Many Inuit knew so little about the world of the *qallunaat* that they believed the War was a battle between the Hudson's Bay Company and a rival company.

"Praise ignorance, for what man has not encountered he has not destroyed," wrote Wendell Berry.

Back to Ernie Riddell. He paced back and forth on his makeshift runway, constantly scanning the sky for a plane. Having notified the police about the murders, he probably wondered if he would become the next Satan?

Ernie especially dreaded trips to the outhouse. The path was exposed, and the outhouse was quite a distance from the trading post.

One evening there was a tapping at the door of the Hudson's Bay Company store on Tukurak Island. Rifle in hand, Ernie opened the door, and a smiling Inuk greeted him, saying, "I have some seal meat for you, Mr. Riddell."

The smiling Inuk was Simeonie's father. Simeonie said Ernie was so relieved by this visit that he stopped carrying around his rifle.

At last the Mounties found a decrepit single-engine Norseman resting on mothballs in Ottawa, repaired it, equipped it with skis, and flew it to Great Whale River, then on to the Belchers.

As the plane was landing, the Qiqiqtarmiut gazed up at it in amazement: most of them had never seen an airplane before. A few thought it might be an unusually large bird, but what kind of bird?

From this presumed bird emerged men dressed in scarlet tunics—Mounties.

"I don't like flying in an airplane," Simeonie told me. "You can't see the world around you like you can in a kayak."

In 1961, every hunter in the Belchers paddled a kayak, according to ethnographer Milton Freeman. Forty years later, Simeonie was probably the last of the Qiqiqtarmiut to travel in a kayak.

Simeonie's grandfather once paddled his kayak several hundred miles south, to James Bay. The reason? "Just to see," Simeonie told me.

The Qiqiqtarmiut helped the Mounties locate the bodies of the murdered Inuit, "A ghastly sight," wrote one of the Mounties, "with frozen blood painting their flesh."

On April 15, RCMP Inspector D. J. Martin—one of the tunic-clad visitors—dispatched a telegraph message from the Belchers to Ottawa in which he stated that nine Inuit had been killed "in the islands," and that the presumed murderers had been taken into custody.

The murderers in question cooperated with the police. Why wouldn't they? The Mounties were feeding them so heartily that they probably associated white man's justice with hearty meals. . . .

Probably none of the islands' new visitors had ever listened to their own borborygmus. This word refers to the gurgling sound made by the layers of muscle in one's intestines squeezing the food that isn't there. A rare sound among white people, but a common one among the Qiqiqtarmiut. . . .

28

From my notebook: I have a roommate, a Canadian government official. In three days, I haven't exchanged more than a few sentences with him because of his devotion to his PalmPilot. If I want to communicate with him, should I walk over to the school and email him?

On the virtues of conversation: you don't have to purchase any sort of device, so you don't need to turn yourself into a consumer, and then—with rapid upgrades in technology—a frenzied consumer.

"One hair of my beard is more dear to me than all the money that can be extracted from me," wrote English naturalist Llewellyn Powys.

On the defects of digital consumption: A person buys data owned by a megacorporation, which then can poke its mega-snout into that person's life.

"What are Facebook and Google but giant corporations?" wrote Nicholas Carr in *The Shallows*.

At one point, my roommate said (without looking up from his PalmPilot), "Sorry about what happened to New York."

As for what happened during the winter of 1941, the Canadian government decided to hold the trial in the Belchers. For they wanted to show all of the Qiqiqtarmiut, not just the accused killers, that murder is not kindly regarded in Canada.

"White people don't believe in killing other human beings," a Mountie informed an Inuk who'd killed several of his fellow Inuit in the early 1920s. The Inuk had heard about the Great War, so he told the Mountie: "I think you believe in killing other human beings much more than we Inuit do."

On August 18, 1941, the judicial party, led by the Honorable Justice C. P. Plaxton and accompanied by several journalists, arrived in the Belchers after a two-week schooner journey from southern Hudson Bay. They would have come earlier, but no airplane could be found to transport them.

"I don't suppose you've ever heard of a Judge Plaxton," I asked my roommate. Strange to say, he now looked up from his PalmPilot. "I know a Plaxton, but the guy's a sanitary engineer, not a judge," he said.

Later I googled "Judge Plaxton" and learned that a man by that name had been a judge in the Barbados in the 1730s.

"Almost 50 Eskimoes smilingly greeted the party on its arrival," reported James McCook of the *Canadian Press*.

McCook also noted that "Adlaytok, one of the accused men, greeted Constable George Dexter affectionately, throwing his arms around the RCMP officer."

A large RCMP tent became the courtroom, with the bewigged Judge Plaxton seated at a table draped with the Union Jack. Behind the judge was a large photograph of the Royal Family.

Nobody in the Belchers would have known why the judge was wearing a thick wig. Maybe it was to keep a polar bear's jaws from crunching his skull?

Facing the judge, the jury, and the suspects were the Qiqiqtarmiut, most of whom were seated on sealskin mats and dressed in eider duck skins.

At the time, eider duck skins were the most common item of wearing apparel in the Belchers. This prompted one of the reporters to write that he felt like he was seated among "a group of man-birds."

Eider duck garb, observed Robert Flaherty, is "to white man's nose . . . most obnoxious."

Most obnoxious to the Qiqiqtarmiut were white man's diseases. Soon after the arrival of the judicial party, they began suffering from influenza, and at least one person—Keytowieack's widow—died from it.

The six-person jury included a mining executive, a mining prospector, two newspaper reporters, a ship's engineer, and Ernie Riddell, but it did not include any of the Qiqiqtarmiut.

There were seven accused: Aleck Apawkok and Akeenik, jointly charged with the murder of Sara Apawkok; Peter Sala and Adlaytok, jointly charged with the murder of Keytowieack; Ouyerack and Qarak, each charged with the murder of Ikpak; and Mina, charged with multiple murders.

Mina had been diagnosed as insane, which made her unfit to stand trial, but not unfit to attend the trial, so she was carried into the tent strapped to a stretcher. Her periodic screams would provide a high-pitched counterpoint to the legal proceedings.

"The fellow who should be punished is the one who gave those Eskimoes a book which white men have been quarreling over for 2,000 years," observed a trapper in Great Whale River at the time of the trial.

On August 19, 1941, Judge Plaxton slammed down his gavel, and the trial began.

29

My roommate and his beloved PalmPilot have returned to Ottawa. A great relief, for he had threatened to have the TV fixed. . . .

Just as (in the words of Russian poet Alexander Pushkin) "a dead man can't live without a coffin," so a twenty-first-century man/woman/child can't live without a screen.

Even as his lift was waiting to transport him to the airport, Mr. PalmPilot was fingering his device. Possible message fingered into that device: "Thank God I'm returning to a place where broken TVs are fixed."

In Sanikiluaq's Northern Store, I was drinking a cup of coffee when a teenage boy wandered over to me and said, "How's it goin', Rambo?" then gave me a poorly executed high five. "The name's Big Belly," I informed him.

I investigated the store's DVD bin and noticed that *The Towering Inferno* was no longer there. A purchase inspired by 9/11?

On films: According to one of Sanikiluaq's grandsons, Flaherty's lost Belcher footage had a scene where his grandfather easily outruns a team of fast-running sled dogs.

"My mother told me that my granddad liked to do somersaults in the snow," the grandson said. "*Nuannarpoq*—that describes him."

Nuannarpoq is an Inuit word that means "to take extraordinary pleasure in being alive." There is no equivalent in English.

At the end of his life, Sanikiluaq suffered from narcolepsy and was forced to hold his eyelids open with his fingers—a sad fate for a person who felt such esteem for the physical world.

I recently googled "Sanikiluaq the man," and one of my first hits was "Book your Man to Sanikiluaq flights with Expedia and find great deals. . . ." ("Man" is an abbreviation for Manchester, England.)

From my notebook: Snow, wind, and frigid temperatures, but I see more smiling faces than I saw in relatively balmy weather. Does seemingly undesirable weather make life in the North more desirable?

Or do the Qiqiqtarmiut make no distinction between good and bad weather? After all, Arthur Twomey called them "an out of door people."

"I'm surprised that you still have your nose," Taliriktuk grinned. For it's a joke among the Inuit that the noses of *qallunaat* fall off as soon as the temperature goes below freezing.

During one snowstorm, I watched the wind blow the snow upward from the ground—seemingly impossible behavior for snow.

During another snowstorm, a man approached me, removed a soapstone carving of Donald Duck from inside his parka, and showed it to me. "That's not traditional," I said. "Yes, it is," the man replied, "I saw it on TV."

Since the sale of carvings is a primary source of income for many of the Qiqiqtarmiut ("No carvings, no smokes," as one man succinctly put it), I bought the Donald Duck carving. I'll give it to some Disney-loving kid, I told myself.

Several days after I purchased it, I looked more closely at the Donald Duck carving and noticed that it had a remarkably realistic eider duck's body attached to its cartoonish head. Sometimes tradition, like beauty, confuses the eyes of the beholder.

30

As I would soon be going home, I offered the old woman several large bills for all the help she had given me. Pushing the bills away, she told me that memories, whether good or bad, have nothing to do with money.

I gave Simeonie my pocket knife. "I must pay for it," he told me. *No!* I exclaimed. "There are two things that a person must pay for—a knife and a dog," he said, "or the knife will be lost, and the dog will die."

Simeonie's payment to me: a pair of warm mittens that he'd made from a dehaired walrus skin.

I checked my emails a final time. I felt warm walking to the school but cold sitting in front of a computer. That's because muscle activity is our body's most important source of heat, and if you're butt-stapled to a screen, you barely move, and your temperature goes down, down, down. . . .

"We're having an anthrax scare," a friend emailed me, "so make sure you don't bring any spores back from Hudson Bay."

Our nervous systems reputedly receive an endorphin reward cue (the adrenaline surge that so pleased my Cyberian friend) every time we receive an email, but I did not receive a reward cue, endorphin or otherwise, upon being told not to bring back spores from Hudson Bay.

Nor did I receive any sort of reward from my lady friend's email informing me that her mother had just been diagnosed with severe arthritis and was now on several types of medication.

I said good-bye to all the elders who had been my informants, no, "informant" is an ugly word that suggests giving privileged information to the police, so I said good-bye to the elders who had become my friends.

I slipped an envelope with cash in it under the old woman's door. I did not identify myself as the source of that cash, but only wrote the word *nakurmiik*, which means "thanks," on the envelope.

One last exchange of words with Jacky: "That attack on New York—you will soon find out that it was a movie," he told me. "But I heard the fires are still burning in New York," I said. "That's what they want you to think, those movie people," he replied.

Taliriktuk could always be counted upon to inject a note of humor into any conversation I had with him, but in saying good-bye to me he now gave me a silent, wordless hug.

At last I decided to say good-bye to Peter Sala.

As I was walking toward Peter's current residence, the cold air gave me goose bumps, an attempt by my body to raise a protective hair cover that it no longer possesses.

The previous time I visited Peter, he was covered by *Cladonia* lichens. He was still covered by *Cladonia* lichens, but now those lichens were covered with several inches of snow.

At the base of Peter's simple white cross was a plaque with these words: "Peter Sala Born Feb 1900 died Jan 26, 1988. Rest in Peace." On the grave was a wind-damaged wreath of artificial flowers.

A blur of white a hundred or so feet away—a snowy owl had swooped down and grabbed a lemming.

The owl's sonar-like ears would have heard the lemming scritching around under the snow from a hundred or more feet away.

Peter's body would have given grease to Flaherty Island's nutrient-deprived soil, which would have responded by producing a local bounty of plants, whose roots would have been eaten by lemmings, which would have been gobbled up by snowy owls.

Snowy owl with lemming

An owl's stomach acids aren't strong enough to digest bones, feathers, teeth, claws, or hair, so it vomits them up in the form of cylindrical pellets.

Those pellets would have offered a substrate for a keratin-inhabiting fungus called *Onygena corvina*, which would be eaten by various small insects and mites, which in turn might be eaten by the predatory mite *Stratiolaelaps scimitus*, all thanks to Peter.

"When we try to pick out anything by itself, we find it hitched to everything else in the universe," wrote John Muir.

Concerning the broken laptop on Camsell Island: Centuries may pass, but not even the most culinarily versatile mite will ever touch it.

Nor will anything else touch it. For the local ecosystem will ask, What's its molecular structure? No answer. For—unlike Peter

Sala—it doesn't have a molecular structure, so it can't be broken down.

"Oh no! Not *another* laptop!" exclaims a visitor to Camsell Island in the year 2285.

And then I said good-bye to the stones, rocks, gravel, and lichen-covered boulders that had provided me with such good company during my sojourn in the Belcher Islands.

31

From the Belcher Islands, I flew to Kuujuarapik, where bad weather, not a terrorist attack, grounded all flights for the better part of a day, so I sat in the small airport and chatted with a local Inuit elder, who called Harold Udgarten "one of the best fiddle players in the Arctic."

Then I flew from Kuujuarapik to Montreal and from Montreal to Boston, where I was greeted by America's remarkably indeterminate post-9/11 warning: "If you see something, say something."

Because of this warning, I expected people to stop each other on the street and say, for example, "Your zipper's down," or "Hey, look at that—there's a contrail in the sky. . . ."

After I got home, I began writing up the first draft of these notes with a pencil (Ticonderoga Tri-Write No. 2).

My friends call me a Luddite, usually with somewhat condescending smiles on their faces, but Luddites were hand-loom weavers, and my abilities as a hand-loom weaver are nonexistent.

Actually, I'm more akin to a Neo-Luddite. In a manifesto drawn up at a 1996 Luddite Conference in Barnesville, Ohio, Neo-Luddism is defined as "a leaderless movement of passive resistance to consumerism and the bizarre and frightening technologies of the Computer Age."

Personal admission: No matter how much effort I put into it, I went nowhere in my attempt to write up my findings on the Belcher murders.

Too much about lichen taxonomy, paper wadded up. Too much about *Nanook of the North*'s inaccuracies, more paper wadded up. Too much bad-mouthing of the Rev. Peck, still more paper wadded up.

I thought about including 9/11, or my experience of it in the Belchers, in the narrative, but discounted the idea.

Why did I insist on writing a detailed account of Camsell Island's geology?

Some writers have reclaimed their inspiration from a change in scenery. For example, Belgian playwright Maurice Maeterlinck rented an abandoned monastery in France and danced around its empty cloisters on roller skates, the better to energize his lethargic Muse.

I checked into a Vermont friend's log cabin, where I soon became engaged in an overlong psychological analysis of both Mina's religious frenzy and Ouyerack's Jesus fixation. Yet more paper wadded up.

The more I wrote, the less I wrote.

"Give it a rest," my lady friend suggested. And so I did, for almost a year.

When I returned to the story, I devoted several not particularly relevant pages to the life of Wetalltuk, the Inuk who drew the map of the Belcher Islands for Robert Flaherty.

I analyzed Wetalltuk's oft-repeated benediction "May your life be rich with seals" despite the fact that its meaning was obvious.

Why did I also write at length about the various fungal species that I'd found in the Belchers? After all, this was supposed an account of a strange religious cult in the Arctic, not a treatise on Arctic mycology.

Some Inuit believe that if you put a small stone in your mouth and suck on it, you will be able to concentrate as you've never concentrated before, so I sucked on a variety of small stones, but with no apparent result.

I googled "suck on stones" to find out if I might have done my sucking erroneously, and among my first hits was "Kidney Stone Humor on Pinterest."

Taliriktuk had recently gotten email, or rather his daughter had gotten him email, and he now sent me this message in English: "America's okay now, I hear not falling down, good to know."

But America was making other countries fall down. Having illuminated the skies over Afghanistan, the rocket's red glare was now illuminating the skies over Iraq.

At the same time, public beheadings seemed to have become digital crowd-pleasers. In 2004, the second most popular Internet video—after *American Idol*—was the beheading of American engineer Nicholas Berg in Iraq.

The visit to Johnny Inukpuk, Nanook's cousin, did not succeed in jump-starting my account of the Belcher murders.

My notebook began gathering dust. Meanwhile, Mark Zuckerberg had invented Facebook, which permitted someone, anyone, to inform the rest of the world, "Whoo-ee, I'm no longer constipated!"

Whoo-ee, here comes Twitter, Myspace, LinkedIn, Instagram, Pandora, Friendster, Tumblr, Pinterest, Snapchat, etc.

My notebook continued to gather dust until the summer of 2012, when an incident with a polar bear blew all the dust away.

32

I've always been more interested in *tupilaks* than other supernatural beings like angels, werewolves, the Blessed Trinity, Osiris, Zeus, Bigfoot, or even the Buddha . . .

. . . so when I heard from a kayaker friend that a *tupilak* attack had caused the East Greenland village of Ikateq to be evacuated, I had no choice but to hop a series of increasingly smaller planes until I arrived in Tasiilaq, East Greenland's metropolis (pop. 1,800).

Carved from bone by an *angakok* or perhaps just a remarkably pissed-off individual, a *tupilak* usually has gaping mouthparts, grasping appendages, and sometimes a skull with a bird beak or two sticking out of it.

Tupilaks have a not uncommon habit of appearing at their victims' windows and smiling sarcastically at them.

Tupilak *peering through a window.*

Regardless of how it looks, a *tupilak* comes alive by suckling its creator's breast or, in certain instances, his penis, then launches into attack mode. Its specialty is pulling out and eating its victim's entrails.

Another personal admission: In the 1980s, I did ethnographic work in and around Tasiilaq, then called Angmagssalik, and preferred its scruffy hunter-gatherer culture to my own resolutely nest-fouling one.

Shortly after I arrived in Tasiilaq, I noticed that it had become a mecca for Chinese tourists, especially those Chinese tourists who (prejudice alert!) would rather look at their LED screens than at Greenland.

"Greenlander?" one of the LED-gazing tourists smilingly asked me, maybe because my disheveled rigging identified me as a local. Before I could answer, the man took my picture.

Several of the Chinese were wearing surgical masks. "Because of pollution," one woman informed me, seemingly mistaking Greenland, which is pollution-free, for her homeland, which is sometimes called "Airpocalypse."

No, I lie: Greenland isn't pollution-free. Or rather its waters aren't. Along with heavy metal particles and organochloride pesticides, toxic compounds from discarded cell phones and computers have entered those waters from the waters to the south.

A peculiar layer in the geologic record will have future hominids scratching their heads and wondering why humans so thoroughly trashed the environment during what's now commonly known as the Anthropocene Era.

Perhaps those future hominids will replace the binomial *Homo sapiens* with *Homo insapiens*.

Now back to the *tupilak* attack. An elder from whom I'd once collected old stories told me this: "A long time ago, a *tupilak* shaped like a walrus and wearing womens' breeches came ashore in Sermiligaq, but I never heard of one in Ikateq."

During our conversation, the elder asked me this question: "Last year American seals killed Osama bin Laden—how?"

The elder knew about actual seals, but not about Navy SEALS, so he didn't understand how my nation's pinnipeds could have managed a journey to an inland country like Pakistan.

A Danish tour operator took me to Ikateq in his fiberglass outboard motorboat. Along the way, we saw several ringed seals and one bearded seal, but not a single Navy SEAL.

In Ikateq, there were no Navy SEALS, either. But I did see evidence of the American military's World War II airbase, named Bluie East Two, in the form of rusted oil drums and rusted boilers.

Whatever you might think of the U.S. military's activities in foreign parts, one thing is true: it refuses to clean up after itself.

The village had indeed been abandoned . . . not only by American soldiers, but also by Greenlanders, most of whose houses seemed to be in a state of collapse. A few houses had rotting dogsleds in front of them.

I searched around for signs of a *tupilak* attack—perhaps a yanked-off arm here, perhaps a partially eaten intestine there.

A middle-aged Greenlander came out of one of the few intact houses (his summer house, it turned out) and asked me what I was looking for. Signs of a *tupilak* attack, I said.

The man laughed. "The only *tupilak* attacks you'll find nowadays are in video games," he told me.

Then what about all the empty houses? "The people here moved to the big city [Tassilaq] mostly because they wanted TV reception," the Greenlander said, adding: "and, of course, they wanted Wi-Fi, too."

On the trip back to Tassilaq, I had the following thought: an attack by a *tupilak* is a much healthier way to make a village one with Ninevah and Troy than the absence of Wi-Fi.

33

When I was last in Tasiilaq in the late 1980s, there were no cafés of any sort, much less Internet cafés. Nor did I hear anyone utter the word *qarassasiaq* (a computer, lit. "little artificial brain") during any of my previous visits.

Now there was an Internet café. I went into it, sat down in front of a little artificial brain, and googled "Ikateq." Among my first hits was "Get Ikateq Greenland Prayer Times."

In the same Internet café, a woman—the daughter of a man from whom I once collected old stories—showed me photos that she'd taken with her cell phone camera of the snow-capped mountains across Tasiilaq Fjord. I could look out the café's window and see those same mountains.

A Greenlandic kid seated at the computer next to me was eagerly working on his avatar—a tall, blond white guy who seemed to like killing short, non-blond guys. . . .

"Wi-fi seems to have killed off all the *tupilaks*," I remarked to Robert Peroni, an Italian living in Tasiilaq.

"But it hasn't killed off the *qivitoqs*," Robert said, then told me about a reputed *qivitoq* attack on a house just down the road from where he lived. The *qivitoq* had smashed through a window and attempted to make off with a young child.

A *qivitoq* is a mountain hermit who possesses the ability to fly as well as the ability to change himself into a polar bear at a moment's notice. He likes to eat children, presumably because their flesh is far less tough than the flesh of adults.

In this instance, the *qivitoq* ended up flying back to his mountain home . . . without the child. So why didn't he stick around and try to get another child?

"Because—even though he liked to eat humans—he couldn't stand their company," Robert smiled. "He preferred the company of mountains."

Toward the end of my trip, the following incident occurred: a Greenlandic teenager was sitting on the shore just outside Tasiilaq and texting when she was approached by a polar bear. At the last minute, the girl saw the bear and screamed, and the bear loped away.

A person. A screen. The person lost in that screen. Along comes Nature in the form of a polar bear. "Ignore me at your own peril," Nature says. The person survives by recognizing Nature.

The incident carried with it this message: you can't write about the Belcher murders without also writing about the screen-driven lives around you. Each represents a particular world coming to an end. . . .

Presto! the dust vanished from my notebook.

34

Shortly after I got back from East Greenland, I was seated in a train rumbling over Boston's fog-shrouded Charles River. It was a scene worthy of Winslow Homer, but twelve people seated in a row were oblivious to it—they were bent over their iDevices as if in prayer.

"I fear technology will surpass our human interaction." Albert Einstein once observed. "The world will have a generation of idiots."

Screened devices > ease of use > mental torpor > mental decline > idiocy.

An example of idiocy: for some reason, a Cyberian ventures out-of-doors, happens to see a bird, mammal, or reptile, and wonders what video game it escaped from.

In the not-so-distant future, the only recognizable mouse will belong to a computer. A mouse harvesting seeds on an autumn this-tle? Too weird!

Even now, a number of Cyberians are more likely to recognize Cloud as a computer term than to identify a type of cloud. Cirrocumulus? What's that?

I gave a talk about the Belcher murders at a small college in New Hampshire. During this talk, a student raised her hand and said: "I just found Ernie Riddell on Facebook—he's now a member of the Royal Vancouver Yacht Club."

Ernie Riddell had been dead since 1989.

The teacher told me: "During a class last week, I conducted an experiment and told my students to put away their computers and iDevices. After they put them away, I saw their fingers working imaginary keyboards and imaginary mice, and by the end of the class, two of them seemed to be hyperventilating."

I mentioned taking the students on detox field trips to some natural setting as a possible remedy against digital overdoses. "A weekend away from a computer?" the teacher said, shaking his head. "That's like rearranging the deck chairs on the *Titanic*."

Cyberia's inhabitants aren't just young people. In a New York restaurant, I saw four so-called senior citizens affixed to their iDevices. They weren't talking or even grunting at each other like our *Austalopithecus* ancestors presumably did.

Nor were they eating the food on their table. Had they replaced food with digital technology?

A man in his late seventies, the father of a friend, told me that he wakes up five or six times during the night, and each time he checks his emails.

Cyberia's inhabitants aren't just seniors and young people. On a Boston street, a middle-aged man talking into his Bluetooth accidentally whacked me with one of his wildly gyrating arms, then gave me an astonished look that seemed to say: And here I thought I was the only person on this planet!

Increasingly, I dream about relocating to Ikateq, where, instead of the low-flying satellites that bring Internet reception, there are low-flying northern wheatears (*Oenanthe oenanthe*) . . .

. . . and where, yes, there might be rusting man-made artifacts, but there are also sculptures of frost-cleft gneiss as well as hummocks blanketed with *Cladonia* lichen and arctic heather, not to mention wispy, creeping Northern Lights, the night sky's own systole and diastole.

35

The first of the Belcher trials began without incident.

Example of an incident: In an earlier Arctic trial, an Inuk shouted *kiliariat* [narwhals], and the Inuit attending the trial quickly ran for their rifles. The judge heard only the word "kill," and he tried to hide under the Union Jack–draped table, lest he be killed.

In his opening address to the court, Judge Plaxton observed: "A people must naturally be viewed in the light of their environment, and the conditions under which they have lived."

The judge followed this seemingly enlightened statement with another in which he appeared to be defending the accused Inuit: "The somber gloom of these island tundras is not conducive to excessive gentleness."

Well put, Your Lordship, I might have thought if I happened to be a liberal outsider attending the trial . . .

. . . but if I was a local Inuk, I might have disagreed with the phrase "somber gloom," which is a lot like Monsieur de Poncsins's "brown monotony" quoted earlier. For if a person has developed an intimate relationship with a tundra habitat, it would not seem sombre, gloomy, or in fact monotonous.

"Lonely and lost was this land", wrote explorer-author Hassoldt Davis about one of the remote places he'd visited, "but it was like a room of one's own."

An example of "somber gloom:" Markassie had been flown to Montreal for what turned out to be only a slightly irregular heartbeat. When he first saw Montreal, he said, he wanted to go back immediately to the Belchers, since there was so much concrete and so little (in his words) "unkilled land."

Like the judge, Crown Prosecutor R. Olmstead wanted to put the Qiqiqtarmiut in their proper context. In his own opening address, he stated: "I contend that it is unfair to treat as equals these members of an aboriginal race who, up to 25 years ago . . . had never seen a white man."

Translation: The Belcher Inuit aren't as intelligent as white people, but now that they've encountered us, they will start advancing up the mental ladder.

Later the crown prosecutor informed the court, "The Eskimo is still a child."

I asked Taliriktuk what he would do if I called him a child. "I would send you to an eye doctor," he laughed. At the same question, Simeonie was not quite as amused. "I would call you a *tukikangitok* [a fool or a retard]," he told me.

36

In the first trial, Aleck Apawkok and Akeenik were accused of killing Sara because she was Satan. The court asked them whether they really thought she was Satan. At the time, *ee* [yes], they replied, but not anymore.

A man named Jonasie, Sara's brother, complained that Sara didn't do "any kind of work around the snowhouse," doubtless, he observed, because she was under Satan's influence.

Do you still think she was under Satan's influence? the court asked Jonasie. He paused for a moment, then said, "I now think she was just lazy."

Judge Plaxton started speaking like the crown prosecutor, referring to the Qiqiqtarmiut as "childlike," "primitive," and "of low mental growth by our standards."

After the judge observed that neither Aleck or Akeeniak had had "religious guidance," the jury retired. Some of the Qiqiqtarmiut misinterpreted their departure and thought they headed out to go goose hunting. They had to be restrained from leaving the tent to go goose hunting themselves.

A short time later, the foreman returned with these verdicts: "Aleck Apawkok and Akeenik, not guilty by reason of temporary insanity."

The verdicts were translated into Inuktitut, but the "man-birds" probably wouldn't have understood a verdict of "temporary insanity" any more than they would have understood why Judge Plaxton wore a wig.

I asked the old woman what she thought of the temporary insanity verdicts. "I don't remember," she said, shaking her head. She possessed the virtue of being elderly.

In a wooded area outside Boston, I recently found a Forked Blue-curl (*Trichostema dichotomum*), a plant in the mint family whose smell, Thoreau said, fed his spirit and "endeared the earth" to him.

When I told a botanist friend at a Boston university about finding the *T. dichotomum*, he shook his head and pointed to his computer. "I don't need to remember Latin binomials anymore because I've got this baby," he smiled.

The baby-owning botanist did not possess the virtue of being elderly.

"If there's a major storm . . . and your Internet connection is out and the batteries on your computer and iPhone have run down, do you know anything?" wrote Naomi Baron in *Words Onscreen*.

An uncomfortable piece of information: Those who spend excessive amounts of time seated at their computers can expect a 15–25 percent shrinkage in the area of the brain that processes memory, speech, and sensory information.

According to Jared Diamond, the Fore of New Guinea can identify 1,400 plant and animal species . . . without the aid of a computer.

In Kuujjuaq, Nunavik, I once did a fungal inventory, and an Inuk brought me a specimen. "We have this," I told him. He pointed to the hairs on the stem, which in fact indicated that this was a species we didn't have.

The Inuk knew nothing about fungal taxonomy, but he possessed the ability to observe.

Mosquitoes don't need to be observed—they can always be discerned by their bite—and since August is a prime mosquito month in the Belchers, I can imagine the judicial visitors slapping at these tiny celebrants of warm-blooded life and saying to themselves, This is a trial in more ways than one.

How many of Mina's shrieks and cries might have come from the fact that she was strapped to a stretcher and unable to slap at the mosquitoes biting her?

37

Next came the trials of Qarak, Adlaytok, and Ouyerack.

The first witness was Mosee, Mina's husband. He said Ouyerack had told him to kill Ikpak, since he, Ikpak, was Satan. "But I didn't want to kill a person like myself," Mosee stated.

Ouyerack told the court that he did not think of Satan as a person like himself. Rather, Satan was an "*ijuruq* [ghost or phantom] who can jump into anyone, even a *piaraq* [baby]."

Since the *atiq* (soul) of an animal, any animal, can also jump into a person, even a baby, Satan's jumping abilities were hardly unique.

Adlaytok, who had killed Keytowieack, admitted that he knew very little about Satan, except that he, Satan, was "*piunngituq* [very bad]."

Before Keytowieack's Bible readings, none of the other Qiqiqtar-miut knew about Satan, either. But they had their own very bad beings, such as . . .

. . . the *kukulingiat*, which emerge from the ground to slash at people with their myriad claws, and the ever-hungry *katintayuuk*, a creature that boasts a huge head and, in lieu of a mouth, a female vulva that swallows unwary members of our species. Let's not forget man-eating eider ducks, either.

Such creatures carry with them this underlying message: do not underestimate the power of Nature. . . .

Judge Plaxton seemed to understand the risk of having a diabolic being in one's camp. If you think another person is Satan, he told the court, "then by doing away with him, you are doing away with a wrongful thing."

Satan's jumping ability would seem to include video games. At a recent creationist conference in Phoenix, Arizona, Christian video game developers blamed Satan for the failure of their products. They tried to perform an exorcism at the conference, but failed.

Satan hasn't interfered with video games in Singapore, where 90 percent of the children are myopic because they spend so much time playing video games.

"My son spends the whole day playing video games," a woman told me. She was from New Haven, Connecticut, not Singapore.

I told the woman with the video game–playing son about the Belcher murders. "Terrible," she said while texting someone.

I also told the texter's husband about the Belcher murders. Immediately, he googled "Belcher + murder," then proceeded to read me a story about the Kansas City Chiefs linebacker Jovan Belcher, who in 2012 killed his girlfriend, then himself.

Qarak was accused of killing Ikpak with bullets "borrowed from Jesus." This caused a titter among several of the jurors.

The crown prosecutor asked Qarak whether he still believed Ikpak was Satan. He shook his head. He said that the Rev. Neilsen had made him see the *manirtaq* (light, lit. "lamp wick").

When I mentioned Qarak's name to a Cyberian friend, she laughed. "Qarak is a popular video game character called the Dark Wanderer."

But Qarak didn't become any sort of wanderer, dark or otherwise. The jury gave him a suspended sentence. He was such a good hunter that, in the words of the Judge Plaxton, "he will hunt for the families of the other prisoners if his sentence is remitted."

"Ayeeh!" shouted Qarak when he learned that he wasn't going to be executed by the *qallunaat* or—just as bad—exiled away from the Belcher Islands.

Adlaytok was a considerably less successful hunter than Qarak, so the court sentenced him to a year's imprisonment with hard labor at one of the RCMP garrisons on the mainland.

Almost nothing is known about Adlaytok's life from that point on . . . except that, according to the Mountie records, he had a very difficult time living away from the Belchers.

38

At the beginning of his trial, Ouyerack wore Peter Sala's bowler hat, presumably to make a good impression on Canada's legal representatives, but the judge asked him to remove it.

Inuit testimony indicated that Ouyerack believed that he was not only Jesus Christ, but also the Holy Ghost. Upon being asked who the Holy Ghost was, Ouyerack replied, "Some friend of Jesus."

"My body was Ouyerack, but my thoughts were Jesus," Ouyerack told the court, adding, "I was very happy being Jesus."

Jesus, like Satan, seems to have been a talented jumper. "Anything, even Jesus, can take possession of your insides," one of the witnesses informed the court.

"Did you give Adlaytok a bullet so he could shoot Keytowieack?" the court asked Ouyerack. Yes, he admitted . . . because he thought Keytowieack was Satan. He did not think Keytowieack was Satan now.

Such a plethora of Satans! the *qallunaat* visitors to the Belchers must have thought.

By comparison, the Salem witchcraft trials could claim only one Satan, described by the pivotal accuser, a Native American woman named Tituba, as a well-dressed, white-haired man from Boston, then later as a dark-haired man from Maine.

In an article for the *Toronto Star*, William Kimmon, a journalist who was one of the jurors, wrote that the Belcher murders were like "a new regime wiping out the old, because Keytowieack was 'the former religious boss on the islands.'"

Neither the judge or the chief prosecutor asked Ouyerack, one of the two new religious bosses, if he had ever been nailed to a cross. If they had, he probably wouldn't have understood the reference. For his only knowledge of wood would have been the drift logs that frequently wash up on the Belchers.

Nor did the end of the world, so often referred to by Ouyerack, Peter Sala, and Mina, come up during the trial.

But the end of the world—again, the natural world—did come up recently in a bar in Hingham, Massachusetts, one of whose numerous TVs displayed the perpetually burning fire on the so-called Fireplace Channel.

The virtue of this sort of fire, the bartender told me, pointing to the large plasma TV, is that you don't need to worry about a real fire, and there's no need to chop wood.

If artificial fires end up replacing genuine ones, it will no longer be possible to roast chestnuts, barbecue ribs, or burn evil politicians at the stake.

In the same bar, I overheard one Cyberian say to another: "Yeah, I've got a 2015 Corvette Stingray with a carbon fiber body and a 40 LTE connection to GM's OnStar driver service network. It's a gigantic rolling smartphone!"

Recommendation: Any person found to be in possession of a gigantic rolling smartphone should be charged with obscenity.

"I am not Jesus anymore," Ouyerack told the court. "I am only a poor Inuk whose name is Ouyerack."

39

Markassie's uncle attended the trial, and when one of the journalists raised his camera and began taking photos of the "man-birds," his uncle became scared.

"He thought the man was shooting at us with some sort of strange *qallunaat* rifle," Markassie told me.

Judge Plaxton cited a recent incident where a Cree man had shot another Cree man because he mistook his victim for a cannibalistic wendigo. The tip-off—wendigos smell very bad, and his victim also smelled very bad.

Like *tupilaks*, wendigos can assume a variety of shapes and forms, but they almost always seem to have a skeletal appearance and possess antlers.

The Cree man received a verdict of manslaughter rather than murder, since—according to the judge—this was a case of mistaken

Wendigo

identity. The analogy was obvious: killing a wendigo and killing Satan were not dissimilar . . .

. . . even though the former was a native species and the latter a noxious invasive.

The last wendigo died in 1962, or so the story goes. Reputedly, he (it?) stood in front of the train to Churchill, Manitoba, believing that the train would stop for him, a supernatural being, and then he would be able to eat the passengers. The train ran him over. *Sic transit gloria mundi!*

The jury in Ouyerack's trial retired and came back a short time later with this verdict: the accused would be sentenced to two years' imprisonment with hard labor in Moose Factory, Ontario, and would not be allowed to return to the Belchers.

"Moose Factory?" asked a Cyberian acquaintance to whom I mentioned the Belcher murders. "Do they manufacture moose there?"

Before I could say that "factory" refers to the jurisdiction of a factor (trader), especially a factor with the Hudson's Bay Company, the Cyberian had hauled out his iDevice and disappeared down the Internet rabbit hole.

40

Since 9/11, Americans had been waiting diligently for another terrorist attack. At last, on April 15, 2013, two bombs fabricated from pressure cookers exploded near the finish line of the Boston Marathon, killing three people and injuring at least 260.

I was camping in northern New Hampshire at the time, and I didn't learn about the bombings until I returned. "You mean you didn't have any contact with the outside world?" a neighbor asked incredulously.

But I'd had plenty of contact with the outside world. My feet had touched numerous granitic outcroppings, and I had seen moose footprints in the snow, tiny yellow cup fungi in balsam fir resin, and mourning cloak butterflies, not to mention the constellation Ursa Major resting contentedly in the sky.

I returned the day after the so-called lockdown, when Boston area residents were obliged to stay indoors, or they might be attacked by the still rampant bombers.

It's an exaggeration, but not much of one, to say that most of those residents would have remained indoors anyway.

"The indoor life is the next best thing to premature burial," observed Edward Abbey.

I asked one of my neighbors how she occupied herself during the lockdown. "I updated my Facebook profile and shared some of my photos on Flickr," she told me.

A paradox: Social media are no more social than Narcissus gazing at his own image in a pool of water.

Another neighbor said she played monster-featured video games with her kids the entire day? *The entire day?* I asked in disbelief. Yes, she said, they really love monsters. . . .

In spite of purveying a rich variety of monsters, screens domesticate our species no less than our species turned a once fearsome canid into a creature that fetches tennis balls, sits placidly in laps, rolls over, and plays dead.

Given our lives of continuous connection, members of our species now have the ability to be everywhere at once, which makes us similar to St. Augustine's God—a being so all-encompassing that he, too, is everywhere at once.

If you're everywhere at once, you're also nowhere at once and, as a result, have no contact with (there's that crucial phrase again) the outside world.

Silicon Valley legend Kevin Kelly once referred to the Internet as "a magic window" that provides "a spookily godlike" perspective on existence, adding: "We can see more of God in a cell phone than in a tree frog."

Given how they are worshipped, digital devices like cell phones ought to be called iGods.

Wait! Kevin Kelly is not a legend. Here's an actual legend, from Greenland: the Moon disguised himself as a handsome seal so he could sleep with his sister, the Sun. When the Sun realized that she had slept with her own brother, she began running, and the Moon began running after her . . .

. . . and that's why night follows day.

Just as—according to the Rev. Jerry Falwell and Pat Buchanan—God was responsible for 9/11, a surprising number of people thought the Supreme Being was behind the Marathon bombings.

A tweet from a church outside Boston: "God sent the Marathon bombs for the sin of Massachusetts passing same-sex marriage."

Prejudice: Only birds should be allowed to tweet.

The two Marathon bombers learned to build explosive devices from the online magazine of the al-Qaeda affiliate in Yemen.

A digitally-savvy twelve-year old with a laptop and a hormonally derived grudge probably could have worked out a far more destructive urban Armageddon than the Marathon bombings.

Passionately in love with digital technology, our species has become its own predator.

41

Peter Sala's trial took place the following day, on August 20, 1941.

"Will God Be Hung?" asked a headline in a Canadian newspaper at the time of the trials.

Several anthropologists have referred to the Belcher murders as a prophet movement, with a prophet/visionary, Peter, proclaiming the imminent transformation of the world.

But Peter was trying to transform the world only insofar as he thought the killing of a certain evil spirit in a tiny portion of that world, the Belcher Islands, might improve it.

"Is Satan present in this courtroom?" the crown's prosecutor inquired. Peter did not open his eyes. "*Nakka*," he said. Which means no, emphatically.

If the Belcher murders were made into a movie, Peter's behavior during the trial would have to be changed, since no actor can win an Oscar or even an Oscar nomination by being silent or by keeping his/her eyes closed during the entire movie.

The Cyberian who thought the Belcher murders would make a terrific movie later changed her mind and told me that "I don't think children freezing to death would attract much of an audience."

British documentary film-maker John Grierson—a good friend of Robert Flaherty's—had gotten permission to film the murder trials, but the remoteness of the Belchers as well as persistent bad weather made it impossible for him to travel there.

It was Grierson who, in writing about Flaherty's second film, a South Seas drama titled *Moana*, coined the word "documentary."

Speaking of films: Cyberians have developed the habit of watching them on their Android devices. Perhaps they get a sense of superiority by observing minuscule members of their own species?

"I'm really worried that my son will turn into the Android he's always using," a woman told me. "He thinks of life as just a giant cradle-to-grave app."

The son in question had a real-life model. "I'm so attached to my computer that I'm really upset when I see that reality doesn't display the time in its upper right hand corner," his father told me . . . only half in jest.

But here's piece of information that's not amusing: Unaware of the outside world while they're gazing at their iDevices, Cyberians are becoming unaware of the world around them even when they're not gazing at those devices. They still blindly walk into each other, lampposts, garbage cans, and even traffic.

Citing an earlier murder case by a Native person, Judge Plaxton told the jury that Peter "was not in a responsible condition of mind" at the time of the killings, and thus he recommended a verdict of manslaughter rather than murder.

The jury retired again. This time there was a somewhat longer wait, perhaps because Peter—being God—was regarded as a primary force behind the Belcher murders.

By now the Qiqiqtarmiut would have realized that juries don't interrupt a trial to go goose hunting, so they remained seated while the jury deliberated.

Peter nodded slightly after the jury foreman returned and announced the following verdict: "Peter Sala, charged with inflicting grievous bodily harm on Keytowieack, sentenced to two years' imprisonment with hard labor."

Like Ouyerack, Peter would be exiled from the Belchers for the remainder of his days.

This relatively mild verdict, the same as Ouyerack's, indicates that Canadian jurisprudence had a rather liberal attitude toward

Native wrongdoers at the time . . . especially if those wrongdoers did wrong to each other rather than to white people.

Peter, Ouyerack, Adlaytok, Aleck, and Akeenik, were escorted by the Mounties to their boat, the *Fort Charles*, and placed in the boat's hold.

As for Mina, she struggled against the Mounties so violently that she was placed in an improvised strait jacket and hoisted onto the boat in a sling hung from the boat's derrick.

On the morning of August 21, 1941, Judge Plaxton and the judicial party left the Belcher Islands on a police plane, and that same afternoon the *Fort Charles* steamed south to Moose Factory, which would be the new home of the exiled Qiqiqtarmiut. For a while.

Shortly after the trial, the *Toronto Star* journalist wrote: "To judge from the actions of the five Eskimoes, no one would have thought they had deliberately and in cold blood disposed of eight [actually nine] other Eskimoes."

The Cyberian who'd disappeared down the Internet rabbit hole when I mentioned "Moose Factory" informed me: "My first hit was 'Find Moose Factory Singles!' But there don't seem to be any Moose Factory singles. . . ."

42

A new record—sixteen people belonging to various races and nationalities (Cyberia's human diversity is unequalled!) seated in a row and gazing into or thumbing their digital devices.

Occasionally, evolution tends to move backward rather than forward. For example, opposable thumbs gave our species the ability to manipulate a wide variety of objects, but those thumbs now seem to be manipulating only mobile technology. . . .

In disbelief, I counted again, but this time there were only fifteen in a row . . . since one of the Cyberians had just gotten off the train.

Recent studies indicate that the brains of Internet addicts contain almost the same amounts of abnormal white matter as the brains of alcohol and drug addicts.

And like addictive drugs, digital-type devices create their own demand. That's because the buyer is already hooked on the product . . .

. . . like a birder friend of mine. Using an app on his iDevice, he succeeded in identifying a semipalmated plover on Cape Cod's Sandy Neck beach in six minutes, while it took me less than a minute to identify the same bird using my app-free guidebook.

Undaunted, my friend told me that he would soon be getting an app for flowering plants, too.

Another example: So riddled with anxiety was the teenage Cyberian when she lost her cellphone that she scratched her face and arms until they bled and, unaware she was bleeding, continued to scratch herself even more.

The girl happened to be the daughter of another friend. "It's not the end of the world," my friend said to her, referring to the lost phone. "Yes, it is!" the girl cried.

Many Cyberians can no longer function without their devices. An example: An e-businessman's smartphone had all his travel information on it, including the name of his hotel, so when he left that smartphone in his hotel, he had no idea where he was staying, and he wandered the streets of Philadelphia, lost.

Remember the genetic modification of arctic char isolated on Tukarak Island? Sitting continuously behind desktop computers could eventually give our own species a zigzag morphology, while the constant use of iDevices could make us resemble chickens pecking at their feed . . . or slouched-over corpses.

Corpses, by definition, are dead to the world.

43

Mina's own posture remained supine while she was flown from Moose Factory to Toronto, and then taken to a psychiatric hospital for examination.

While she was sedated, Mina was baptized by an Anglican priest. *Sedated?* Perhaps the priest was taking no chances with a person who had been responsible for the deaths of six people.

Anglican missionaries specialized in baptizing Inuit who suffered from tuberculosis or some other disease. Such sufferers were usually not inclined to reject Christianity . . . especially if the missionaries accompanied the baptism with medication.

The Rev. E. J. Peck frequently referred to Christ as "The Great Physician" while administering to the Inuit. I can imagine him telling a would-be acolyte something like, "The Anglican faith will cure that hacking cough in no time."

There were exceptions, of course. Like Canon Webster of Coppermine, in the Northwest Territories. In the 1950s and 1960s, he pulled hundreds of Inuit teeth without ever referring to Christ as "The Great Dentist."

The priest who baptized Mina later claimed that she was "undoubtedly of superior intelligence compared to many of the natives we have contacted in the past."

"Superior intelligence": could this mean a willingness to adopt white man's habits, particularly his religion?

While she was in the hospital, Mina was learning English. One of her first sentences in the new language was: "I want to help you." She was probably repeating a statement she heard from the priest who baptized her.

Help! exclaims our species . . . and iDevices come to the rescue. There's now a wearable computer-type item called a Pavlok. You strap it to your wrist, and it delivers a mild electric shock that says, hey, it's time to hit the gym or pick up the kids at day care.

As it happens, Apple's helpmate Siri didn't die in a car crash. Rather, she's become a genie who, with the help of a so-called HomeKit-connected device, turns off or on lights, opens doors, checks thermostats, etc.

By the time you read these words, the Pavlok and HomeKit devices will have become outmoded, perhaps replaced by—what? An iPhone app that will tell you right away if you have bad breath?

Maybe IBM's ongoing attempt to make a smartphone that will approximate all five human senses?

Rhetorical question: How many other similarly gratuitous electronic beasts are currently slouching toward Silicon Valley to be born?

When such runaway growth occurs in an organism, it's called cancer.

After she became a new person, Mina was put in a plane and flown back to Moose Factory, where she joined the other Belcher exiles in attending Anglican church services every evening and three times on Sunday.

Peter Sala refused to speak with Mina before her conversion, but he began speaking with her again once both of them became enthusiastic churchgoers.

Mina would soon turn her statement of "I want to help you" into something akin to an assault.

44

In 2014, I flew to Timmins in northern Ontario, then took a bus to the town of Cochrane, then a rickety train through boreal forest and muskeg to Moosonee, and then a boat to Moose Factory, a Cree village resting so low in the lowlands of Hudson Bay that parts of it are periodically flooded.

A spring flood once carried away the St. Thomas Anglican Church—where the Belcher Inuit prayed—and it had to be towed back. Due to ongoing water-damage, the church is now condemned.

"At first we were afraid of them," a Cree elder named John Trapper told me, referring to the Belcher Inuit. "We walked past their tents [at the RCMP compound] each morning on the way to school, and we thought, Will they kill us? Soon we realized they were just the same as us."

Another elder, a man named Jimmy Wesley, remembered the Belcher Inuit. "They were always smiling," he told me, "except the tall one."

"The tall one" would have been Peter Sala.

Peter was immediately put to work chopping wood for the Mounties, carrying stones for the roads, and winching the *Fort Charles* and other ships in and out of the Moose River.

"I want to show you something," Jimmy said. Whereupon we walked over to the Moose River, then bushwhacked through ferns, horsetails, purple vetch, and especially giant hogweed (*Heracleum mantegazzianum*).

Originally from the Caucasus Mountains, giant hogweed is an alien plant that has outcompeted local plants in many parts of Canada . . . just as the Christian God, an alien deity in the Canadian North, has outcompeted local deities.

Now Jimmy pointed to a badly rusted winch a few feet away from the giant hogweed and directly above the Moose River. The tall one was always working with it, he said. *Always*, he repeated.

Might Peter have thought of this sort of continuous work as an antidote to grief?

Jimmy's family name used to be Wabajun, which means "Whitewater," since one of his ancestors delighted in paddling his canoe in frothy, roaring rivers. A perfectly sensible name . . .

. . . but the newly arrived Anglican missionaries in the nineteenth century did not have an easy time pronouncing Cree names, so they renamed Jimmy's grandfather—along with many of the other local Cree—Wesley, after the Anglican divine John Wesley.

Since it was lunch time, we sat down beside the Moose River, and Jimmy brought out a tin of Klik and some bannock to go with the apples and oranges I had bought at Moose Factory's Northern Store.

I was familiar with bannock, a type of unleavened bread quite common in Canadian outposts like Moose Factory.

Bannock is the substrate (so to speak) for this oft-told Cree joke: What did the trapper who'd spent his whole life in the bush say when he saw his first pizza? Answer: Who barfed on the bannock?

But I had never heard of Klik. Later I googled it, and rather than tell me that it was the Canadian version of Spam, Wikipedia provided me with this tidbit of information: "In computer programming, Klik or Click is a game development RAD tool using visual programming."

Question: Can you spread a RAD tool on bannock?

A Canadian version of Spam doesn't sound very tasty, but I've often thought that the flavor of food depends on the physical setting where it's eaten, and so it was that with the gray-blue Moose River eagerly rushing past us, and Canada jays and ravens perched in the nearby trees, my Klik tasted just fine. . . .

45

"Take the Indian out of the child" was a quote commonly used in Canada by proponents of residential schools.

From the 1880s until the mid-1980s, Native children in Canada were snatched from their families and forced to attend schools usually presided over by gentlemen of the cloth who were often anything but gentle.

Like John Trapper, Jimmy Wesley attended the Bishop Horden Residential School. One morning he stopped and tried to talk with Akeenik ("new girl in town," he said), but they could only manage a series of gestures, since Cree and Inuktitut are quite different languages.

"I tried speaking to her in English, but that didn't work, either," Jimmy said.

Jimmy was so late to school that his teacher, an Anglican minister, clubbed one of his hands . . . clubbed the hand repeatedly and so hard that, he said, "I still have almost no feeling in it seventy years later."

Jimmy's prominent cheekbones and wide nostrils made him seem perpetually alarmed, as if he could not get the minister's violent act out of his head.

Concerning Bishop Horden, the school's namesake: In 1855, two years after he arrived in these parts, Horden, then only a missionary, delighted in the fact that he had already baptized eighty-two of the local Cree.

Along with performing baptisms, Horden and the other missionaries informed the Cree that eating food with cutlery—likewise using a napkin at mealtimes—was essential for their salvation.

In the old days, Jimmy said, many Cree were baptized by Anglican ministers, then rebaptised by Catholic priests, and then baptized all over again by the Anglicans. "We must have gotten very wet," he added.

Jimmy also told me this: upon noting that the Cree fought off disease by wearing moose tooth charms, Anglican missionaries gave the Cree seemingly less primitive charms to fight off disease—Holy Bibles and crucifixes.

I asked Jimmy what he remembered about Akeenik. "She always had a cut lip," he said, by which he probably meant she had the congenital fissure known as a harelip.

Also: "She sewed clothes for our people out of coats and trousers the Mounties had thrown away. My father owned a parka she made for many years. It was a very nice parka, too."

We were now joined by Jimmy's wife, Anna. "That woman, we called her Agnes, she had tuberculosis," Anna said. "I worked in the hospital's TB ward, Ward 3, where she was a patient for many years. I remember that she liked to sing 'Jesus Loves Me.'"

I wondered: Did Akeenik/Agnes think of what she had done to Sara Apawkok while she was singing this hymn?

Tuberculosis, caused by the bacterium *Mycobacterium tuberculosis*, was once so rampant in the Canadian North that missionaries distributed samplers with "Don't Spit" written in large letters to Native people, although most of the recipients of these samplers couldn't read.

The missionaries could also have distributed samplers with "Don't Talk" written on them, since talking is just as likely to spread the bacterium as spitting.

How had the bacterium arrived in the North? Most likely, it was brought there by early white visitors like those missionaries themselves.

Ouyerack spent most of his time coughing, wheezing, and gasping for breath in his tent. "We almost never saw him," John Trapper told me, "but we always heard him."

A local doctor visited Ouyerack and determined that he was suffering from tuberculosis. In his case, pulmonary tuberculosis.

Akeenik seems to have had the extrapulmonary variety, because Anna told me that she sang "Jesus Loves Me" without punctuating the words with coughs.

In January, 1942, a perpetually coughing Ouyerack was admitted to Moose Factory's new thirty-two-room hospital. The first night he slept in the hospital was probably the first night he ever slept in a structure made from anything other than snow, sod, or animal skins.

Ouyerack died on May 27, 1942. Postmortem tests for tuberculosis turned out to be negative. In permanent exile from the Belchers, could he have willed himself to die?

"Our native soil draws all of us, by I know not what sweetness, and never allows us to forget," wrote the Roman poet Ovid, himself an exile.

46

In Moose Factory, I visited the St. Thomas Anglican Church's cemetery with John Trapper. We were accompanied by a number of exuberant *misasaks,* an insect that breeds promiscuously in the Hudson Bay lowlands.

I had written the first few drafts of these notes by hand, but I'm now using my computer to write this final draft as a Word file, and the spellcheck keeps changing *misasak* to "missal."

Little does a computer know that *missal* (there it goes again!) is the Cree word for a large northern horsefly, which, in the words of an early visitor to the Canadian North, "lands on you with a thump, takes a bite out of your flesh, and then retreats to a nearby tree, where you can hear it masticating."

Slapping at the *misasaks,* John and I wandered around the cemetery. Most of the grave markers were wooden crosses with no names on them. Several of those crosses were also broken. One of the broken crosses had only a single legible word on it: "Beloved."

Names on the gravestones: several Highboys, a few Smallboys, a number of Wesleys, and a single Butterfly.

The Smallboys, John told me, were almost all over six feet tall.

John showed me a large concrete cenotaph that listed the names of the Inuit from the east coast of Hudson Bay who'd been shipped to the Moose Factory hospital and died without being cured of whatever ailed them, which was usually tuberculosis.

Ouyerack's name was on the list, with the designation E9-541 next to it.

Why such a designation? Because white outsiders had an even more difficult time with Inuit names than they had with Cree names, so the Inuit received numbers, and by those numbers they were subsequently known.

Inuit dog tag

For many years, every Canadian Inuk was obliged to wear his or her identity number engraved on a dog tag and worn around the neck. Dog tags worn in the western Arctic began with a "W," while those worn in the eastern Arctic, like Ouyerack's, began with an "E."

Not only Inuit names, but Inuktitut itself perplexed most *qallunaat*. When they did try to speak it, the results were often mixed, as when a clergyman in Igloolik in the 1950s confused *ijjujut* (Bible) with *igujut* (testicles) and told his congregation that they should be paying more attention to their testicles.

John and I gazed at one cross after another, but we couldn't find a cross that marked Ouyerack's final resting place.

If Ouyerack had actually been Jesus, he would have risen shortly after he died, but—like Peter Sala—he went down rather than up, thus becoming a part of the local ecosystem.

Roseroot (*Rhodiola integrifolia*) is a cold climate plant that usually doesn't survive in more temperate zones. In the unmowed cemetery, I noticed a bountiful patch of it.

If Ouyerack had been buried near this patch, perhaps it was his latter-day descendent . . .

. . . or perhaps the roseroot was the descendant of a Cree man named Sinclair Whitefish whose grave was very close to it.

All at once John was reminded of something else about the Belcher Inuit: "They were afraid of trees."

Unlike the Belcher Islands, Moose Factory is situated below the tree line, so if you visit the village and its environs, you'll see black and white spruce, balsam fir, poplar, tamarack, and several different types of birch—hardly frightening at all.

But here's something that *is* frightening: many deciduous trees in different parts of the world are developing fissures on their bark and even shedding that bark as a result of, it's assumed, Wi-Fi radiation.

"We travel the Milky Way together, trees and men," wrote John Muir.

47

At the Cree Interpretation Center in Moose Factory, I met a middle-aged man everyone called Upsagan. This nickname refers to a bracket fungus, *Fomes fomentarius*, that Mark Wesley (his actual name) frequently uses as a fire starter in the bush.

"I like getting down and dirty with nature, and I can't do that with a lighter or matches," Upsagan told me.

I asked him what inspired his delight in dirt. He told me: "My grandmother was dying. She said, 'Don't look at me. Get out of the house and look at the world.' And so I did . . ."

Another specialty of Upsagan's: drying the membrane that cloaks a moose's capacious heart and making tote bags out of it.

Eager to have the membrane around a moose's heart as a carrying conveyance, I bought one of his bags, and as of this writing, it has done splendidly in all kinds of weather.

"If it's obsolete, it works," wrote mountaineer-explorer H. W. Tilman.

Upsagan told me of an incident he'd heard about from his father: One day Peter Sala escaped from the Mountie compound, stole a canoe, and began paddling. The Mounties apprehended him at Charles Island . . . and put him back behind the winch.

In a motorized canoe, I set off for Charles Island with Upsagan and his eleven-year-old son. The son played Nintendo for the entire trip.

Pointing to a small cove with a campground and a purple port-a-loo directly above it, Upsagan said, "I think the Mounties must have captured your friend [Peter Sala] right over there."

I'd told Upsagan about the Belcher murders. Now he told me about an incident that occurred fifty miles east of Moose Factory, at a place called Hannah Bay. In 1832, a group of starving Cree asked the local Hudson's Bay Company man for food. The HBC man refused to give them food unless they gave him furs.

"Not unusual behavior for a Company man," I remarked. To which Upsagan replied: "But it gets ugly . . . like your story."

"*Yes!!!*" Upsagan's son shouted not in agreement, but at his Nintendo handheld video system.

"The Cree shaman contacted the Great Spirit, and he said, 'Kill the bastards!' Upsagan continued. "So they killed nine people at the post, even some half-Cree servants."

"Sounds like he contacted the Christian God," I remarked, swatting at a mosquito.

"Probably true," said Upsagan, "because I don't think we had a Great Spirit in those days, only lots of nature spirits, and they never would have told us to kill our fellow human beings."

One of the elders at Moose Factory told me this story: Shortly after the arrival of the first missionaries, some Cree killed a whiskey jack (Canada jay) and decided that if the bird's gizzard caught a fish, they would become Christian.

The gizzard caught one fish, then another, and then another, so they said good-bye to the animistic past and converted to Christianity.

"Some people say they've heard the cries of the dead at Hannah Bay," Upsagan added, echoing what Markassie had told me about the dead children on Camsell Island.

We hauled the canoe ashore in the cove where Peter was captured. It was only a short distance from Moose Factory, so Peter probably would have been captured before he could manage a smile.

But I managed a smile, albeit an ethnographic one, when Upsagan pointed to an *Usnea* lichen (Old Man's Beard) dangling from a black spruce and told me that Cree women once used it as a feminine hygiene absorbent.

While the St. Thomas Anglican Church's cemetery in Moose Factory bred giant horseflies, Charles Island bred mosquitoes and did so in such quantities that it made most other places seem mosquito-bereft.

I've noticed that mosquitoes in different places have different-pitched whines. Here, for instance, the whine had a relatively low pitch that sounded a lot like the sacred Hindu syllable *om*.

In the Canadian North, a case can be made for the mosquito as a true conservationist, determined at all costs—often sacrificing its very life—to preserve wild lands from invasions by resource sniffers and developers.

Another point in favor of these miniature conservationists: As soon as baby birds break free from their eggs, usually in the late spring, they begin snapping up mosquitoes, an extremely important source of nutrition for them.

Upsagan wanted to burn an *upsagan* to keep away the whizzing, stinging hordes of mosquitoes, but we couldn't find his namesake fungus on any of the islands' trees, so we coated our exposed body parts with DEET (N, N diethyl-meta-toluamide), a much less healthy alternative.

Seated at a picnic table, the two of us were talking (his son, seemingly impervious to the bloodsuckers, continued to play Nintendo) when all of a sudden there was a very strong gust of wind.

Without looking up, Upsagan said, "Balsam poplar . . ."

. . . and then he added: "Not so long ago, our people could identify a tree by the sound the wind made in its branches. Now there
are only a few of us who can do it. So much is being lost. . . ."

So much is being lost. The balsam poplar above us seemed to whip its
branches up and down in agreement.

48

Whether Ouyerack died of tuberculosis will probably never be known, but one person who did die of TB was a nineteenth-century Concord, Massachusetts, resident named Henry David Thoreau.

Quite a few Concordians did not appreciate Thoreau. There was once an old lady who often put flowers on Ralph Waldo Emerson's grave in the town's Sleepy Hollow Cemetery, but who muttered as she passed Thoreau's, "And none for you, you dirty little atheist."

Back from Moose Factory, I was foraging for mushrooms very close to the dirty little atheist's grave, and I found several *Suillus* species, symbiotic partners with the nearby white pines. Yet another example of how, in Nature, everything is hitched to everything else.

Like Peter Sala, Thoreau was hitched to the local ecosystem. In his case, he was well aware of the fact. He wrote: "Pines and birches or, perchance, weeds and brambles, will constitute my second growth."

I was collecting the *Suillus* mushrooms for later consumption (not surprisingly, graveyard mushrooms taste very good) when a voice called out to me from a SUV on one of the cemetery's roads: "Hey, buddy. My GPS crapped on me. You know the way to Route 2?"

I gave the voice directions without consulting a GPS.

A short while later, I heard the word "Hello?" spoken loudly over and over again, like a broken record at full volume. A man's cell phone seemed to have crapped on him, and he was wandering among the gravestones, even occasionally wandering into them.

Hello, hello, hello, says a person on his/her cell phone. *Tap, tap, tap,* goes another person on his/her computer keyboard. Meanwhile, a supermall rises up on the last bit of wild land in the vicinity . . .

. . . or another Burger King/McDonald's/Kentucky Fried Chicken/ Subway is squatting obscenely on a recently drained wetland.

Mr. Hello now walked over to me. "Hey, you got a cell phone I can borrow?" he asked. I told him I didn't own a cell phone.

The stressed expression on Mr. Hello's face indicated that not only had his god failed him, but he couldn't find a replacement god and thus had become the technological equivalent of an atheist.

"It's so open here, I was trying to get a satellite connection," he said when I asked him why he was in the cemetery.

Opinion: It's much better to get a connection with the ground on which you're standing than with an artificial object thrust high into the sky.

Earlier in the afternoon, I'd visited Walden Pond because a friend had told me about a great horned owl perched in a tree there, and I hoped to find an *Onygena* fungus growing on one of its pellets.

You might recall the species in question, *Onygena corvina*, from my visit to Peter Sala. It doesn't grow directly on the pellet, but on the bones of the small mammalians gulped down by the owl and then vomited up in the pellet.

Onygena corvina on owl pellet

Personal admission: I would rather find an *Onygena Corvina* on an owl pellet than a bag of gold pieces.

I didn't locate the owl, but I did see a large milk snake with alternating bands of red, black, and yellow slithering across the trail directly in front of two kids who were so affixed to their iDevices that they didn't notice it.

Contrary to popular belief, our grandchildren won't condemn us for what we've done to the planet because they'll be so lost in the solipsism of the tech-dependent world that they won't notice it (i.e., the planet).

"A thing is right when it tends to preserve the integrity, stability, and beauty of the biotic system," wrote environmentalist Aldo Leopold. "It is wrong when it tends otherwise."

Where are the Aldo Leopolds, the Rachel Carsons, the John Muirs, the Barry Commoners, the Loren Eiseleys, the David Browers, the Teddy Roosevelts, and the Edward Abbeys now? Lurking behind screens rather than being out in the field, what's left of it?

Rant: A computer is only a tool, but so, too, is a guillotine.

Person after person I've watched lose their heads in a realm of total busyness because of their computers and iDevices. "I have to answer more than 200 emails a day," a Cyberian professor recently told me, "but there's nothing I can do about it."

Meaning: I'll never be able to escape this gulag.

In the Siberian gulags, a small pink flower in the spring would bring prisoners to the point of ecstasy, whereas prisoners in the Cyberian gulags seldom notice flowers regardless of their color or season.

If you don't see Nature, why would you want to preserve it?

49

C omputers are like Old Testament gods; lots of rules and no mercy," wrote mythologist Joseph Campbell.

No mercy: Either you believe in me, a computer declares, or else you believe in me.

I recently gave a lecture on Arctic ecology at a local junior college and, as usual, most of the students were paying attention to their iDevices rather than to my lecture, so I changed the subject . . .

. . . and asked my audience in a suddenly loud voice: "Do you realize that many drakes lose their penises because female ducks mistake them for a postcoital snack?"

Hardly anyone looked up, laughed, winced, seemed dumbfounded, or even said "cool," awesome," or "ohmigod," currently three of the most often used words in the English language, for their iDevices were saying to them, "Look at me, for I am God."

Oral tradition is as much about listening as it is about telling stories . . . and listening, like storytelling, seems to be going the way of the dodo and the passenger pigeon.

After the class, the teacher took me out for lunch, but I lost my appetite when she informed me that the school's library would soon be getting rid of all of its books and going completely digital.

I'd lost my appetite because of similar revelations before. For more and more libraries are retreating to a pre-Gutenberg age (i.e., before 1450) by dumpstering their books.

When I was at Walden Pond searching for owl pellets, I realized I'd left my pocket knife at the Sleepy Hollow Cemetery. After I returned to the cemetery and retrieved the knife, I approached Thoreau's grave. "Henry David," I said, "I think we're in trouble."

There was no response, but in a nearby tree a white-throated sparrow was singing "Poor Sam Peabody, Poor Sam Peabody," perhaps the saddest of all bird songs.

50

In 1945, Peter and Mina—still considered risky individuals—were relocated to the Nastapoka Islands north of Great Whale River and then, a year later, to the village of Port Harrison on the northeast coast of Hudson Bay.

At the time RCMP Major McKeand wrote: "Transportation of any kind between Port Harrison and the Belcher Islands . . . is difficult summer and winter."

Meaning: regardless of the season, Peter and Mina would find it almost impossible to make their way back to the Belchers.

In Port Harrison, the two Belcher exiles prayed at an Anglican church whose bell the local Hudson's Bay Company factor often rang to summon his employees to a poker game.

Robert Flaherty filmed *Nanook of the North* in and around Port Harrison in 1920–21. While he was making the film, he was also making more offspring. I can imagine Peter and Mina meeting these offspring, who would now be adults, and thinking, There are Flahertys everywhere. . . .

My Eskimo Friends is the title of the book Flaherty wrote about the Belcher Islands as well as the making of *Nanook*. Nowhere in this book does he refer to any of his liaisons with Inuit women. If the book had been more accurate, it might have been called *My Eskimo Girlfriends*.

In 1947, all of the Qiqiqtarmiut almost became exiles, for the Canadian government had a plan to relocate them to the High Arctic, the better to establish its sovereignty there. The plan was never put into action.

If at first you don't succeed, try, try again . . . especially if the issue is sovereignty. In the early 1950s, Canada more or less forced a group of Port Harrison Inuit to inhabit the High Arctic islands that had been designated earlier for the Qiqiqtarmiut.

One of the High Arctic exiles was a man named Josephie, born from Flaherty's union with *Nanook*'s leading actress Maggie Nujarluktuk (film name: Nyla) three decades earlier.

Josephie's designation, in spite of the fact that neither "Josephie" or "Flaherty" would have been hard to pronounce, was E9-701.

Stuck on Ellesmere Island since 1953, Josephie had a mental breakdown in 1968 and died in 1984. He had petitioned the government repeatedly to *please please let me go back home*, but his requests were ignored.

"We were the government's guinea pigs," Rynee Flaherty, Josephie's widow, told a reporter for the *Toronto Star* in 2009.

Rynee's own designation was E9-551.

Robert Flaherty, often referred to as "The Father of Documentary Film," was also the father of no one knows how many Inuit in the Hudson Bay area. He died in 1951 without ever meeting a single one of them.

51

Port Harrison, now called Inukjuak, has so little touristic appeal that it doesn't have any listings, biased or unbiased, on Trip Advisor. Which is a good recommendation in itself.

Another good recommendation: one of Inukjuak's residents once fought off three polar bears with only a wooden tent pole. . . .

The stick wielder was Johnny Inukpuk, Nanook's cousin. In the 1970s, the three bears in question tried to enter his tent, and he wielded one of that tent's poles as if it were a samurai sword, driving them away.

"Those bears didn't seem to be hungry," Johnny told me. "I think they just wanted to meet somebody who thinks *Nanook of the North* is funny."

He meant unintentionally funny. Did I want an example? He mentioned the scene where Nanook bites a phonograph record to determine whether it might be edible . . . despite the fact that, in real life (as opposed to reel life), his cousin owned a record player, albeit one that had a broken spring, so he had to twirl the records with his fingers.

Not funny enough? How about the scene where Nanook heroically battles an already dead seal and at last pulls it up from the ice in a state of advanced rigor mortis?

The future of documentary cinema would probably have been different if *Nanook* had been made by an ethnographer like Franz Boas, Margaret Mead, or Claude Levi-Strauss rather than a self-styled artist like Robert Flaherty. . . .

"Mr. Flaherty thought us Huskies (that's what he called us!) were always fighting against our environment," Johnny told me, "because that's what *qallunaat* do. But we believe in living with our environment, not fighting it."

"We also believe in living with sea ice, or with what's left of it," Johnny added.

Sea ice nurtures the ocean floor. When the algae clinging to the bottom of this ice die, they sink down to feed benthic creatures such as clams. With the loss of ice, the clams are getting less to eat, so they're getting smaller, and the eider ducks that depend on those clams are getting much less nutrition . . .

. . . which is one of the reasons why they're starting to die off in the Belcher Islands, among other places in the North.

Walrus also depend on those clams, with the result that their numbers are plummeting, too.

While I was visiting Johnny, he picked up the long baculum of a walrus and raised it into an upright position, then grinned and said Flaherty's *oosik* (penis) would "go like this" at the sight of an Inuit woman.

Since it's a bone inside the penis, the baculum of a walrus is stiff all the time, a fact that tourists find so amusing that a carved *oosik* souvenir is often the first item they ask for when they meet an Inuit artist.

Carved oosik

A recently dead seal was lying on the floor, and now Johnny went back to flensing it with a briskness that belied the fact that he was in his early nineties.

On the subject of dead things: Johnny owned a television, but he almost never watched it. "I can't see sitting and looking at an *itsivautaq* all the time," he told me.

Itsivautaq means "a piece of furniture."

52

Inukjuak's undeclared but highly visible motto: "My satellite dish is bigger than your satellite dish."

If they were living in Inukjuak today, Peter and Mina could now be eating pork rinds dipped in Cheez Whiz—both available at the local Northern Store—while watching *Duck Dynasty* on satellite television.

Context: The vast microbial domain called Archaea, which constitutes at least half the life on our planet, lies in deep geological strata directly beneath anyone who watches *Duck Dynasty* or anything else on a screen.

Observed Norwegian ecologist Arne Naess, "All organisms are equal: human beings have no greater value than any other creature, for we are just ordinary citizens in the biotic community, with no more rights than amoebas or bacteria."

And, he could have added, Archaeans.

More context: Some of the world's oldest rocks, called greenstone, rest in the ground twenty-five miles south of Inukjuak. These rocks are 4.28 billion years old, whereas Cyberia is hardly more than thirty years old.

I asked Johnny whether he remembered Peter Sala. "He spent his time in the church, and I spent mine in the bush, so we didn't see each other much," he told me.

But he did remember that Peter would sometimes sing "London Bridge Is Falling Down." This English nursery rhyme/song had probably been taught to the Qiqiqtarmiut by Robert Flaherty.

Peter had gone from being God to being a devout worshipper of God. Maybe he thought such devotion would bring him forgiveness, but it brought him only more devotion.

"It is not God but grief that has the advantage of ubiquity," wrote the French-Romanian philosopher E. M. Cioran.

By the late 1970s, Peter had undergone another relocation and was back in Great Whale River. A photograph of him at this time shows an elderly Inuk with a framed painting of Joseph holding the infant Jesus in the background.

In Great Whale, two Anglican priests, the Rev. Tom Martin and the Rev. John Sperry, visited Peter to administer the eucharist, but they found him asleep. They decided not to wake him up, since—as the Rev. Martin later quipped—"it's better to let sleeping gods lie."

If Peter could not live in the Belchers, at least he could die there. In 1982, Canadian authorities decided that an eighty-two-year-old Inuk could not cause much harm, so they granted him his wish, and he was allowed to return home.

For Peter, the events of 1941 were a closed book, one that he never opened again, or he would have doubtless become even more overwhelmed by grief than he already was.

Internet posting on a recent article about the Belcher murders in the Inuit newspaper *Nunatsiaq News*: "I am the grandchildren of Peter Sala. My dad never says to me about the story."

In the years before his death, Peter was still more or less a pariah, even among his own family members. Some of the Qiqiqtarmiut would spit in his direction when they saw him.

The old woman did not spit at him. "When Peter came back here, I forgave him," she told me. "He had already suffered enough."

"I could have stopped all those killings," Peter told Taliriktuk shortly before his death in 1988.

53

Murder in the name of religion has become a trademark of the human species. Shortly after I wrote those words, a presumed Islamic terrorist killed forty-nine people in an Orlando, Florida, nightclub.

Citing 9/11, the Crusades, and the Spanish Inquisition, comedian-philosopher George Carlin stated: "Thou shalt keep thy religion to thyself."

"Hey, let's surf the Web," a Cyberian friend said to me recently, and I was tempted to reply: Keep thy religion to thyself.

"When I'm sitting behind my computer, I feel like I'm in heaven," this same Cyberian once told me.

Speaking of heaven: Many Arctic missionaries promised the Inuit that they would meet God and Jesus in person if they succeeded in making it there . . . and that the seal meat in heaven tasted far better than it did on earth.

"But we only want to do good for them," a minister on Baffin Island told me when I complained about the damage his forebears had done to Natives in the North.

"If I knew for a certainty that a man was coming to my house with the conscious design of doing me good, I should run for my life," wrote Thoreau in *Walden*.

There's another, very different heaven from the one situated somewhere in the sky. A northern Dogrib Indian told a missionary about this realm, as reported by nineteenth-century Arctic explorer Warburton Pike.

The Dogrib man (Pike wrote) asked the missionary if his heaven had musk oxen, flower-covered hills, winds that make you feel like the wind, lakes blue with the summer sky, and nets full of fat whitefish, adding: "If your heaven doesn't have these things, Father, please leave me alone with my land."

I bet you didn't leave him alone with his land, Father!

Despite the claims of certain religious groups, the sky doesn't seem inclined to send us humans signs, portents, omens, messages, symbols, warnings, prophecies, or directives.

It's a pity that Ouyerack didn't simply gaze up at the meteor shower and regard it with wonder . . .

. . . as did nineteenth-century naturalist Alfred Wallace, whose ship had burned and who was drifting randomly in a leaky lifeboat. He wrote: "During the night, I saw several meteors, and in fact could not be in a better position to observe them than lying on my back in a small boat in the middle of the Atlantic."

Nowadays a meteor shower would probably go unnoticed in the Belchers.

In an email he sent me a year or so ago, Taliriktuk wrote, "Everyone here in Sanikiluaq, they're all going digital now, and they don't look at nothing else. Me, too! Haha, I am how you say it screened-in. . . ."

The subtext of Taliriktuk's email: the Belcher Islands, extremely remote only a hundred years ago, had become part of Cyberia and are now no more remote than Paris, London, Moscow, New York, Capetown, Tashkent, Albuquerque, or Peoria, Illinois.

Of what value is a digital device without a blank spot on the map?

Taliriktuq ended his email with the Inuktitut word *ajurnamaat,* which means something like "That's the way it is" or "Nothing can be done about it."

54

There remains Mina. Who, like the missionaries, wanted to help. . . .

A final google: "Mina + help." One of my first hits welcomed me to the Apache Mina site. Since Mina wasn't an Apache, I tried again, and my next hit brought me to the "Mina 2.0 User Guide."

I closed my laptop and opened Johnny Inukpuk. When I visited him in Inukjuak, I asked him if he remembered a woman from the Belcher Islands named Mina. He looked thoughtful for a moment, then said: "I heard she liked *qallunaat* better than her own people."

A mail plane flew to Port Harrison four times a year, and each time it landed, Mina would rush over to the runway and greet it, "waiting for the white peoples' eyes to be turned towards her," wrote Margery Hinds in an article in the Canadian magazine *The Beaver*.

Margery, the Port Harrison schoolteacher, knew Mina reasonably well. "She was a very good housekeeper—clean, punctual, and thorough," she wrote.

But perhaps too good a housekeeper?

Nicknamed "Blitzkrieg Bessie," Mina would descend on the nurse's quarters, the local weather station, the RCMP barracks, or any other *qallunaat* house, and whether or not the occupants wanted their facility cleaned, she would scrub, scrub, scrub away. . . .

She lived in a tent in the middle of Port Harrison, and her only possessions were items that scrubbed, washed, and cleaned.

One of the photos of Mina shows her poised with a vacuum cleaner, a big glimmering smile on her face.

At the time most Inuit wouldn't have used vacuum cleaners, maybe wouldn't have even known what they were, so Mina's use of one was probably an example of her newfound joy in all things *qallunaat*.

Mina would ask the *qallunaat* residents of Port Harrison to take off their clothes not because she felt they should meet their Savior naked, but because she wanted to wash their garments.

Did she believe that cleanliness is next to godliness, or did she instead think cleanliness would wipe away the type of godliness that she'd displayed several years earlier on the ice of Camsell Island?

Mina did not clean the church in Port Harrison, probably because she thought it was by definition clean . . . in spite of the fact that Hudson's Bay Company employees often played poker inside it.

The "poker church" was replaced by a new church in 1965. I paid a visit to this new church in 2005 and, to my delight, I heard the whistling of snow buntings in its rafters.

Opinion: I can't think of a better congregation for any church than a group of snow buntings.

Of course, snow buntings prefer the wild to churches. In 1895, explorer Fridtjof Nansen encountered a snow bunting within five degrees of the North Pole. It flitted cheerfully around him for a while, then flew north. . . .

Another photograph shows Mina dancing happily with a cocker spaniel puppy named Pingua. "Her best friend," a former Hudson's Bay Company man told me, adding: "Maybe her only friend."

But Mina was just as happy to dance without a canine partner. At a party in Port Harrison, she continued to dance by herself long after the music stopped, "like an automaton," reported Margery Hinds.

55

Mina kept on dancing by herself, day after day, month after month, and year after year, until she danced right into the present. . . .

Was Mina one of the nineteen (a new record!) passengers seated in a row on the train, their thumbs working like automatons on their iGods?

Was it Mina whom I recently saw taking a selfie next to a statue of Paul Revere while holding the hand of a toddler who kept repeating over and over again, "Password, password, password . . . ?"

Was it Mina who told me that she felt much worse when her computer crashed than when she had some sort of medical problem?

Did Mina exchange her vacuum cleaner for a computer, sit down, and never get up again?

A week or so after describing this putative Mina's dance into Cyberia, I received an email from Taliriktuk's daughter telling me of her father's death.

All of the other Qiqiqtarmiut who'd talked to me about the 1941 murders had died. Now Taliriktuk, too. His daughter told me that he'd had a massive stroke not long after watching a DVD of *Nanook of the North*.

Taliriktuk's daughter added: "When my dad wanted to learn about our culture, he watched this movie."

Not only had I lost a friend, but I'd lost a friend who'd mistaken the screened world for the real one.

"How shall the heart be reconciled / to its feast of losses?" asked poet Stanley Kunitz.

I decided to reconcile my heart to Taliriktuk's death by doing what I usually do when confronted by a loss—I went for a walk.

I walked until I reached the end of the world, where I heard a white-throated sparrow singing not "Poor Sam Peabody, Poor Sam Peabody," its usual song, but "Bye Bye Nature, Bye Bye Nature," a very different song.

Ajurnamaat. That's the way it is.

GLOSSARY OF INUIT WORDS

angakok (pl. **angakut**)—shaman

atiq—soul

ayee!—wow! or great!

ee—yes

ijuruq—a ghost or phantom

ijurnarunaq—funny, laughable

Inuktitut—the Inuit language

kalopaling—a man-eating eider duck

kamik—a sealskin or bearskin boot

Naakalauk—Big Belly; euphemism for a white person

nanook—polar bear; also the name of the hero in *Nanook of the North*

qallunaak (pl. **qallunaat**)—white person

Qiqiqtarmiut—Inuit of the Belcher Islands (lit., "People of the Islands")

qivitoq—A Greenlandic hermit with a cannibalistic bent

siuk (pl. **siut**)—ear

tupilak—a Greenlandic monster that eats human entrails

ACKNOWLEDGMENTS

Robert Pearson—for his diligent research into the Belcher murder trials and his scholarly essay on the subject

William Closson James—for his discussion of the Belcher murders in *Locations of the Sacred*

Ray Price—for his account of the Belcher murders in *The Howling Arctic*

The Stefansson Library at Dartmouth—for providing me with a typescript of the murder trials

Kim Cheechoo—for connecting me with elders in Moose Factory

Bill Fraser—for helping me with logistics in Sanikiluaq

Gary Moore—for offering a critique of this manuscript

Suzy Hunt—for both her splendid line drawings and her proofreading skills

Gretchen Wade—for her archival expertise

Russell Potter—for his photographs of Robert Flaherty

Rex Passion—for the map of Hudson Bay

Sylvie Cote Chew at the Avataq Cultural Institute—for providing me with photographs